The
Ultimate Little
SHOOTER
BOOK

RAY FOLEY

This publication is designed to provide accurate and authorita-
tive information in regard to the subject matter covered. It is
sold with the understanding that the publisher is not engaged
in rendering legal, accounting, or other professional service. If
legal advice or other expert assistance is required, the services
of a competent professional person should be sought.—From a
Declaration of Principles Jointly Adopted by a Committee of
the American Bar Association and a Committee of Publishers
and Associations

All brand names and product names used in this book are
trademarks, registered trademarks, or trade names of their
respective holders. Sourcebooks, Inc., is not associated with
any product or vendor in this book.

Published by Sourcebooks, Inc.
P.O. Box 4410, Naperville, Illinois 60567-4410
(630) 961-3900
Fax: (630) 961-2168
www.sourcebooks.com

Library of Congress Cataloging-in-Publication Data is on file
with the publisher.

Printed and bound in Canada.
WC 10 9 8 7 6 5 4 3 2 1

This book is dedicated to our son, Ryan Peter,
the best shot we ever took!

ACKNOWLEDGMENTS

To the amazing staff at Sourcebooks, especially Sara Kase, who handled all problems by turning them into solutions. Also for getting the names of a couple great bars in Chicago.

Peter Lynch for his foresight and having great taste in his selection of books.

Dominique Raccah for being Dominique Raccah.

Lauren Saccone for being Lauren Saccone. Check out her blog: www.fearandloathingny.blogspot.com.

All the readers of *Bartender Magazine* and www.bartender.com and all the bartenders in the USA!

Special thanks: Jimmy Zazzali, Matt Wojciak, John Cowan, Michael Cammarano, Marvin Solomon, Millie Rinaldi, Laura Keegan, Meredith and Lindsay Scharf, Linda Saccone, Dave Conroy, Eugene Desimone, Robert Suffredini, Rene Bardel, Peter and Terri Nelson, Hymie

Lipshitz, and the rest of the Foley tribe, Raymond, William, and Amy.

Also to all those who submitted recipes to www.bartender.com and the readers of *Bartender Magazine.*

A SHORT HISTORY OF SHOT GLASSES

BY MARK PICKVET

Tiny glass vessels were once filled with lead shot and were then used to clean and support quill pens. This origin of the word *shot* had its beginnings in Europe. The *shot glass* is an American term for a tiny drinking vessel used for serving whiskey in single measures.

Before the widespread use of the word *shot* in the late nineteenth century, there were a variety of other terms used to describe them. Dram glasses and firing glasses were popular in England dating back to the early eighteenth century. Dram glasses were cheaply made of thin metals and broke easily but were used heavily in the practice of dramming. Dramming involved drinking several small toasts of rum, gin, brandy, or whiskey in succession, ordinarily in lodges, taverns, and even specialty dram shops. Firing glasses were stronger articles of thick glass, particularly the bottoms. They could withstand considerable abuse and were typically slammed bottom up on the table after each successive toast. The resulting noise was comparable to that of a musket firing, hence the name *firing glass*. In America, *toy whiskey tasters* was the term for the first generation of tiny whiskey tumblers because they were so small (most had a capacity of barely an ounce). They date back to the 1830s and were used for sampling whiskey.

One of the most significant eras in shot-glass history began in the 1880s and lasted up to Prohibition when the amendment was ratified in 1919. Before Prohibition, clear or crystal shot-sized glasses were produced as a form of advertising. Naturally the advertising was alcohol-related and intended for proprietors, distillers, store owners selling whiskey, pharmacists and doctors dispensing liquor, and patrons of saloons, clubs, and so on. Salesmen, peddlers, and agents offered free samples of whatever product they were promoting in shot-sized glasses. Other shot glasses were produced in cut crystal and garish carnival colors during the Depression era. A new style of shot glass was made during the 1920s and 1930s; it was 2 ⅞ inches tall, narrower, held exactly one ounce, and had an incredibly thick bottom. But there were some with bottoms so thick their capacity was less than an ounce: customers often referred to them as *cheaters*.

Manufacturers printed popular toasts on shot glasses, such as "Here's Looking at You," "Bottoms Up," "Down the Hatch," "Just a Swallow," and many others. In the post-Depression era, the decorated tumbler soon became the most popular medium for shot-glass production. Machine-applied enamels and heat-transfers were cheaply fused to shot glasses in huge numbers. Shot glasses decorated with advertising, sports teams, Christmas and other holiday motifs, plain patterns, and logos from tourist hot spots have characterized the post-Depression era. Production of thick, durable shot glasses for bar use has never wavered since the time of the firing glass.

INTRODUCTION

All recipes have been alphabetized for your convenience.

Techniques for Mixing

1. Build: Pour one liquor on top of the other, per recipe, so that ingredients mix.

2. Layer: Pour the first ingredient, then hold a bar spoon slightly above it and pour the next ingredient so that the bottom layer is not penetrated. Repeat with each liquid ingredient.

3. Shake and strain: Shake with ice, and strain.

4. Float: Similar to layering, except the floated ingredient is added to a finished drink and, unlike a layer, gradually blends in.

   *We do not recommend flaming any shooter.

All recipes with this icon have been submitted by one of America's top bartenders. Enjoy!

Publisher's Note: This book and the recipes contained herein are intended for those of a legal drinking age. Please drink responsibly and ensure you and your guests have a designated driver when consuming alcoholic beverages.

SHOOTERS FROM A TO Z

43 Nutty Russians

1 part Licor 43
1 part Disaronno amaretto
1 part Absolut vodka

Layer into your favorite-size shot glass.

 FRANK LIPPAY • LEHIGHTON, PA

69er

⅓ oz. Baileys Irish cream
⅓ oz. crème de banana
⅓ oz. white crème de cacao

Shake with ice, and strain into a shot glass.

95 North

½ oz. Absolut vodka
½ oz. amaretto
½ oz. DeKuyper Peachtree schnapps
½ oz. Midori melon liqueur
½ oz. orange curaçao
Splash sweet and sour mix

Shake with ice, and strain into a shot glass.

 TAMI PARKER • DELAND, FL

99 Apples

1 oz. 99 Apples schnapps
1 oz. butterscotch schnapps

Shake with ice, and strain into a chilled shot glass.

99 Bananas

1 oz. 99 Bananas schnapps
1 oz. blue curaçao

Shake with ice, and strain into a chilled shot glass.

99 Blackberries

1 oz. 99 Blackberries schnapps
1 oz. cranberry juice

Shake with ice, and strain into a chilled shot glass.

99 Oranges

1 oz. 99 Oranges schnapps
1 oz. lemon-lime soda

Shake with ice, and strain into a chilled shot glass.

99 Oranges Creamsicle

1 oz. 99 Oranges schnapps
1 oz. vanilla vodka

Shake with ice, and strain into a chilled shot glass.

99 Peaches

1 oz. 99 Peaches schnapps
1 oz. lemonade

Shake with ice, and strain into a chilled shot glass.

420

½ oz. 7-Up
½ oz. energy drink
¼ oz. Hpnotiq liqueur
¼ oz. Malibu mango rum
¼ oz. Midori melon liqueur
¼ oz. Peachtree schnapps

Shake with ice, and strain into a shot glass.

 MICHELE HAGUE • DE ORO MINE COMPANY •
SPRING VALLEY, CA

ABC

½ oz. amaretto
½ oz. Baileys Irish cream
½ oz. Cointreau

Build.

A-Bomb

¼ oz. Baileys Irish cream
¼ oz. Frïs vodka
¼ oz. Kahlúa
¼ oz. Tia Maria

Shake with ice, and strain into a shot glass.

Absente Shot

1 oz. 7-Up
1 oz. Absente absinthe

Shake with ice, and strain into a chilled shot glass.

 O. WILDE • HOBOKEN, NJ

Absolut Aphrodisiac

1 raw oyster
1 oz. Absolut Peppar vodka
Splash Tabasco

Place oyster and vodka in a shot glass. Add Tabasco.

Absolut Firecracker

1 part grenadine
1 part Absolut Peppar vodka
1 part blue curaçao

In a shot glass, layer equal parts in the above order and let the fireworks begin!

Absolut in the Ocean

½ oz. Absolut vodka
½ oz. Cointreau
Splash blue curaçao

 ANDREAS GROUZIS • SKALA KEFALONIA, GREECE

Absolut Nut

¾ oz. Absolut vodka
¾ oz. Frangelico

Shake with ice, and strain into a shot glass.

Absolut Pepparmint

1 ¼ oz. Absolut Peppar vodka
¼ oz. Rumple Minze peppermint schnapps

Mix.

Absolut Quaalude

1 part Absolut vodka
1 part Baileys Irish cream
1 part Frangelico

Shake with ice, and strain into a shot glass.

Absolut Sex

1 ¼ oz. Absolut Kurant vodka
½ oz. Midori melon liqueur
Splash 7-Up
Splash cranberry juice

Pour the first two ingredients into a shot glass.
Fill with equal parts 7-Up and cranberry juice.

Absolut Stress

½ oz. Absolut vodka
¼ oz. Malibu rum
½ oz. peach schnapps
Splash cranberry juice
Splash pineapple juice

Shake with ice, and strain into a shot glass.

Absolut Testa Rossa

1 oz. Absolut vodka
½ oz. Campari apertif

Serve in a shot glass.

Absolut White Death

½ oz. Absolut vodka
½ oz. Chambord
½ oz. white crème de cacao

Shake with ice, and strain into a shot glass.

African Violet

¾ oz. green crème de menthe
¾ oz. Frangelico

Build.

After Burner

¾ oz. Hiram Walker peppermint schnapps
¾ oz. Kahlúa

Shake with ice, and strain into a shot glass.

After Burner #2

¾ oz. Tia Maria
¾ oz. Hiram Walker peppermint schnapps

Build.

After Eight

½ oz. Hiram Walker green crème de menthe
½ oz. Kahlúa
½ oz. half-and-half

Layer and serve in a 2-oz. shooter glass.

After Eight #2

⅓ part Kahlúa
⅓ part Baileys Irish cream
⅓ part white crème de menthe

Build.

After Five

⅓ part Kahlúa
⅓ part Baileys Irish cream
⅓ part Rumple Minze peppermint schnapps

Build.

After Six

¾ oz. Carolans Irish cream
¾ oz. Hiram Walker peppermint schnapps
Splash Kahlúa

Serve chilled in a shooter glass.

After-Dinner Mint

1 oz. dark crème de cacao
½ oz. Baileys Irish cream
Splash green crème de menthe

Build.

Agean Shooter

¾ oz. Metaxa brandy
⅓ oz. grenadine
⅓ oz. ouzo

Shake with ice, and strain into a shot glass.

Agent Orange

½ oz. Grand Marnier
½ oz. Myers's Original dark rum
½ oz. sweet and sour mix
½ oz. Tropicana orange juice

Shake with ice, and strain into a chilled shot glass.

Aggravation

¾ oz. half-and-half
½ oz. Kahlúa
½ oz. Teacher's scotch whisky

Shake with ice, and strain into a shot glass.

Alabama Nut Slammer

1 oz. Frangelico
¼ oz. Southern Comfort

Serve in a shot glass.

 CHRISTOPHER DABBS • HOMEWOOD, AL

Alabama Slammer

¼ oz. Disaronno amaretto
¼ oz. Southern Comfort
¼ oz. Stolichnaya vodka
Splash orange juice
Dash grenadine

Shake with ice, and strain into a shot glass.

Alabama Slammer #2

½ oz. amaretto
½ oz. orange juice
½ oz. sloe gin
½ oz. Southern Comfort
½ oz. vodka

Shake with ice, and strain into a shot glass.

Alamo

1 ½ oz. Southern Comfort
½ oz. grapefruit juice

Shake with ice, and strain into a shot glass.

Alaskan Oil Slick

1 oz. Rumple Minze peppermint schnapps
½ oz. blue curaçao
Jägermeister to float

Shake schnapps and curaçao with ice and strain
into a shot glass. Float Jägermeister on top.

Alaskan Oil Spill

¾ oz. Jägermeister
¾ oz. Rumple Minze peppermint schnapps

Build.

Ali Berry

1 oz. Three Olives berry vodka
¼ oz. 7-Up
¼ oz. Ocean Spray cranberry juice cocktail
¼ oz. sweet and sour mix

Good served frozen, on the rocks, or straight up.

 ALI MCGRATH • SPENCER'S ALI • OSWEGO, NY

Alice in Wonderland

1 oz. Jose Cuervo tequila
¼ oz. Grand Marnier
¼ oz. Tia Maria

Shake with ice, and strain into a shot glass.

All Fall Down Shooter

1 shot Monte Alban tequila
1 shot Myers's Original dark rum
1 shot Tia Maria

Shake with ice, and strain into a shot glass.

Almond Joy

½ oz. amaretto
½ oz. dark crème de cacao
½ oz. half-and-half
½ oz. vodka

Shake with ice, and strain into a shot glass.

Almond Joy #2

½ oz. amaretto
½ oz. dark crème de cacao
¼ oz. Coco López cream of coconut
¼ oz. half-and-half

Shake with ice, and strain into a shot glass.

Almond Smash

½ oz. amaretto
1 oz. crème de almond
1 ½ oz. 7-Up

Build.

Aloha Shooter

½ oz. pineapple juice
¼ oz. amaretto
¼ oz. grenadine
¼ oz. orange juice
¼ oz. Southern Comfort

Shake with ice, and strain into a shot glass.

Alpine Breeze

1 oz. pineapple juice
½ oz. Myers's Original dark rum
½ oz. peppermint schnapps
1–2 dashes grenadine

Shake with ice, and strain into a shot glass.

Altered States

⅓ oz. Kahlúa
⅓ oz. Baileys Irish cream
⅓ oz. brandy

Build.

Alyce from Dallas

1 part Kahlúa
1 part Grand Marnier
1 part Monte Alban tequila

Build.

Amaretto Chill

1 part amaretto
1 part lemonade
1 part pineapple juice
1 part vodka

Shake with ice, and strain into a shot glass.

Amberjack

1 part amaretto
1 part Jack Daniel's whiskey

Build.

American Dream

½ oz. amaretto
½ oz. Frangelico
½ oz. Kahlúa

Shake with ice, and strain into a shot glass.

American Flag

½ oz. blue curaçao
½ oz. cream
½ oz. grenadine

Layer in order.

Amigo Shooter

⅔ shot Kahlúa
⅔ shot Monte Alban tequila
Splash half-and-half
Nutmeg or allspice for garnish

Blend and strain. Garnish with the nutmeg or allspice.

Amor

1 oz. Sauza Conmemorativo tequila
½ oz. Hiram Walker orange curaçao

Build.

Angel Bliss

¼ oz. Wild Turkey bourbon
¼ oz. Bacardi 151 rum
½ oz. blue curaçao

Build.

Angel Wing

1 oz. white crème de cacao
1 oz. Baileys Irish cream

Build.

Angel's Delight

1 part grenadine
1 part Cointreau
1 part sloe gin
1 part light cream

Layer in order in a cordial glass.

Angel's Kiss

1 ½ oz. dark crème de cacao
Dash heavy cream
Maraschino cherry for garnish

Build. Garnish with the cherry on a toothpick.

Angel's Tip

1 shot dark crème de cacao
Half-and-half to float

Add crème de cacao to a shot glass. Float half-and-half on top.

Anti-Freeze

½ Midori melon liqueur
½ Smirnoff vodka

Build.

Anti-Freeze #2

1 oz. blue curaçao
½ oz. spearmint schnapps
Dash 7-Up

Shake the first two ingredients with ice and strain into a shot glass. Top with 7-Up.

Anti-Freeze #3

1 part green crème de menthe
1 part vodka

Shake with ice, and strain into a shot glass.

Apocalypse Now

⅓ oz. Baileys Irish cream
⅓ oz. dry vermouth
⅓ oz. tequila

Shake with ice, and strain into a shot glass.

Apple & Spice Shooter

⅔ shot applejack brandy
2 splashes half-and-half
Cinnamon for garnish

Shake with ice, and strain into a shot glass. Garnish with the cinnamon.

Apple Delight

½ oz. apple schnapps
¼ oz. amaretto
¼ oz. cranberry juice
¼ oz. vodka

Shake with ice, and strain into a shot glass.

Apple Pear Bomb

½ oz. Absolut Pear vodka
½ oz. DeKuyper Sour Apple Pucker
    schnapps
1 can Red Bull

Mix vodka and Sour Apple Pucker into a shot glass. Fill 6-oz. glass with Red Bull (4-oz. can). Drop shot into the glass; shoot immediately.

 RAYANNA CHOJNACKI • SICKERVILLE, NJ

Apple Pie

¾ oz. apple schnapps
½ oz. cinnamon schnapps

Build.

Apple Pie #2

⅔ shot apple schnapps
⅓ shot Frangelico
Dot whipped cream
Allspice for garnish

Pour the first two ingredients into a shot glass. Top with whipped cream and then dust with allspice for garnish.

Apple Sensation 2000

1 ½ oz. Stolichnaya vodka
¼ oz. DeKuyper Sour Apple Pucker schnapps
¼ oz. Midori melon liqueur
Splash cranberry juice
Splash sweet and sour mix

 MATT KAY • LOS ANGELES, CA

Apres Sobieski

2 oz. Sobieski vodka
½ oz. Marie Brizard white crème de menthe

Shake with ice, and strain into a shot glass.

Arctic Front

1 oz. vodka
1 oz. Yukon Jack whiskey

Shake with ice, and strain into a shot glass.

Armadillo

½ oz. Kahlúa
½ oz. Disaronno amaretto
¼ oz. Grand Marnier
¼ oz. Bacardi 151 rum

Build.

Armpit

1 ½ oz. Rumple Minze peppermint
  schnapps
½ oz. Cranberry juice
Splash 7-Up

Shake the first two ingredients with ice and strain into a shot glass. Top with 7-Up.

Asian Persuasion

½ oz. Bacardi 151 rum
¼ oz. Malibu rum
¼ oz. Midori melon liqueur
Splash 7-Up
Splash pineapple juice

 ATHANIE LEEVIRAPHAN • STILLWATER, OK

Assassin

¾ oz. Hiram Walker crème de banana
¼ oz. Hiram Walker blue curaçao
¾ oz. Hiram Walker triple sec

Build.

Atomic Bomb Shooter

1 oz. bourbon
½ oz. tequila

Atomic Green

½ oz. Hiram Walker banana liqueur
½ oz. Hiram Walker peach schnapps
½ oz. Midori melon liqueur
¼ oz. cream
¼ oz. Frïs vodka

Shake with ice, and strain into a shot glass.

Astropop

¾ oz. Goldschläger, chilled
¾ oz. Yukon Jack whiskey, chilled
¼ oz. grenadine
¼ oz. Midori melon liqueur

 MICHAEL KANE • SANTA MARIA, CA

Atomic Shot

½ oz. Goldschläger
½ oz. Absolut Peppar vodka
½ oz. Jose Cuervo tequila
Splash club soda

Build.

 STEPHAN PORTER • LAZY ARMADILLO •
WOONSOCKET, RI

Attitude Adjustment

1 part ouzo
1 part Rumple Minze peppermint schnapps

Build.

Attitude Adjustment #2

¾ oz. Baileys Irish cream
¾ oz. root beer schnapps
¾ oz. Southern Comfort

Shake with ice, and strain into a shot glass.

August Moon

½ oz. amaretto
½ oz. Cointreau
½ oz. orange juice
Whipped cream to top

Shake with ice, and strain into a shot glass. Top
with whipped cream.

Australian Lemondrop

1 ½ oz. Stubbs Australian rum
3 oz. lemon juice
1 oz. sweet and sour mix
Splash 7-Up

Build.

Australian Shooter

1 shot Jack Daniel's whiskey
Splash cola

Build.

Avalanche

½ oz. Kahlúa
½ oz. Hiram Walker white crème de cacao
¼ oz. Southern Comfort

Build.

Avalanche #2

1 part Baileys Irish cream
1 part Jägermeister
1 part spearmint schnapps

Build. Shoot, look over your shoulder once, and down the slope!

 CHRIS LIMA • PORTSMOUTH, RI

Aviator

¾ oz. Dubonnet Blanc
¾ oz. Harveys Bristol Cream sherry

Shake with ice, and strain into a shot glass.

B-12

⅔ oz. Baileys Irish cream
⅓ oz. Grand Marnier

Build.

B-26

1 part Carolans Irish cream
1 part Cointreau
1 part Kahlúa

Shake with ice, and strain into a shot glass.

B-51 in Flight

1 part Kahlúa
1 part Baileys Irish cream
1 part Bacardi 151 rum

Build.

B-52

½ oz. Kahlúa
½ oz. Baileys Irish cream
¼ oz. Grand Marnier
¼ oz. Absolut vodka

Build. Drink through soda straw from bottom up.

B-52 with Bombay Doors

½ oz. Kahlúa
½ oz. Baileys Irish cream
½ oz. Grand Marnier
½ oz. Bombay gin

Build.

B-54

⅓ shot Kahlúa
⅓ shot Baileys Irish cream
⅓ shot Disaronno amaretto

Build.

B-69

¼ oz. Bailey's Irish cream
¼ oz. butterscotch schnapps
¼ oz. Grand Marnier
¼ oz. Kahlúa

 ROBIN NORWOOD • DAPHNE, AL

Baby Ruth

1 part Frangelico
1 part vodka
2-3 peanuts for garnish

Build. Garnish with the peanuts.

Bacardi Coco Cream Pie

1 oz. Bacardi Coco rum
½ oz. half-and-half
½ oz. vanilla rum

Shake with ice, and strain into a shot glass.

Bacardi Grand Melón Ball

1 ½ oz. Bacardi Grand Melón rum
½ oz. pineapple juice

Shake with ice, and strain into a chilled shot glass.

Bacardi Grand Melón Saltwater

2 oz. Bacardi Grand Melón rum
Salt to rim glass

Shake with ice, and strain into a chilled, salt-rimmed shot glass.

Bachelor's Surprise

⅓ oz. Kahlúa
⅓ oz. Southern Comfort
⅓ oz. white crème de cacao

Back Draft

1 oz. Jose Cuervo tequila
½ oz. Grand Marnier
4 dashes Cholula hot sauce

Let the hot sauce settle to the bottom of the shot glass before serving.

 STEVE MEYERS • SOUTHAMPTON, NY

Back in Black

1 part Tia Maria
1 part Chambord

Build.

Bad Attitude

¼ oz. Absolut Citron vodka
¼ oz. amaretto
¼ oz. sloe gin
¼ oz. Southern Comfort
⅛ oz. cranberry juice
⅛ oz. sweet and sour mix
⅛ oz. 7-Up

Shake the first six ingredients together. Top with 7-Up.

 DEBBIE DOUGLAS • DUCKY'S BAR • PONTIAC, MI

Bad Sting

½ oz. anisette
½ oz. Grand Marnier
½ oz. Jose Cuervo tequila
Splash grenadine

Build.

Bah Humbug

½ oz. amaretto
½ oz. cranberry juice
½ oz. orange juice
½ oz. Southern Comfort

Shake with ice, and strain into a shot glass.

Bahama Nut

¾ oz. Nassau Royale liqueur
¾ oz. Frangelico

Build.

Baileys Bomber

¾ oz. Baileys Irish cream
½ oz. J&B scotch whisky

Build.

Baileys Comet

½ oz. Baileys Irish cream
½ oz. Kahlúa
½ oz. vodka
Dash half-and-half
Splash club soda

Shake the first four ingredients with ice and
strain into a shot glass. Top with a splash of soda.

Bald Eagle

1 ¾ oz. Monte Alban tequila
Peppermint schnapps to float

Ball Bearing

1 ¼ oz. champagne
¼ oz. Cherry Marnier

Build.

Bambi

¾ oz. Baileys Irish cream
¾ oz. Kahlúa
¼ oz. Courvoisier cognac

Shake with ice, and strain into a shot glass. Check your sight and shoot! Delicious sipped on the rocks too.

 JAN DEBENEDICTIS • MILLIS, MA

Bambino

½ oz. Disaronno amaretto
½ oz. half-and-half
½ oz. Stolichnaya vodka

Shake with ice, and strain into a shot glass.

Banana Bliss

1 oz. crème de banana
½ oz. cognac

Banana Boat

½ oz. Tia Maria
¼ oz. Kahlúa
¼ oz. Hiram Walker peppermint schnapps
¼ oz. Myers's rum cream

Build.

Banana Boat #2

¾ oz. banana liqueur
¾ oz. Malibu rum
½ oz. pineapple juice

Shake with ice, and strain into a shot glass.

Banana Boat #3

⅓ shot Kahlúa
⅓ shot Tia Maria
⅓ shot Hiram Walker peppermint schnapps
Baileys Irish cream to float

Build.

Banana Boomer

¾ oz. Puerto Rican rum
½ oz. Hiram Walker banana liqueur
¼ oz. orange juice
¼ oz. pineapple juice

Shake with ice, and strain into a shot glass.

Banana Buca

½ oz. crème de banana
½ oz. orange juice
½ oz. Romana sambuca

Shake with ice, and strain into a shot glass.

Banana Popsicle

½ oz. Frïs vodka
½ oz. Hiram Walker crème de banana
½ oz. orange juice

Shake with ice, and strain into a shot glass.

Banana Sandwich

½ oz. Kahlúa
¼ oz. crème de banana
¼ oz. half-and-half
¼ oz. Myers's rum cream

Shake with ice, and strain into a shot glass.

Banana Slip

1 ¼ oz. crème de banana
1 ¼ oz. Baileys Irish cream

Layer in order in a cordial glass.

Banana Split

½ oz. half-and-half
½ oz. Hiram Walker crème de almond
½ oz. Hiram Walker crème de banana
¼ oz. Kahlúa

Shake with ice, and strain into a shot glass.

Banana Split #2

2 parts crème de banana
1 part Kahlúa
1 part Malibu rum
Splash pineapple juice

Shake with ice, and strain into a shot glass.

 THE BRIELLE RIVER HOUSE • BRIELLE, NJ

Banana Surfer

½ oz. banana liqueur
½ oz. half-and-half
½ oz. Malibu rum

Shake with ice, and strain into a shot glass.

Bananarama

1 oz. banana liqueur
½ oz. Bacardi
¼ oz. orange juice
¼ oz. pineapple juice

Shake with ice, and strain into a shot glass.

Bananarama #2

½ oz. Hiram Walker amaretto
½ oz. Hiram Walker crème de banana
½ oz. Kahlúa
¼ oz. half-and-half

Shake with ice, and strain into a shot glass.

Banshee

1 oz. crème de banana
½ oz. white crème de cacao

Shake with ice, and strain into a shot glass.

Bare Knuckles

1 part Bärenjäger honey liqueur
1 part John Powers Irish whiskey

 WILLIAM LAFORGE • WILD ROVER PUB &
RESTAURANT • MANCHESTER, NH

Barney

1 oz. Bacardi rum
1 oz. DeKuyper Grape Pucker schnapps
½ oz. Cointreau
Splash 7-Up
Splash sweet and sour mix

Shake with ice, and strain into a shot glass.

 DAVE ISAACS • ST. CLOUD, MN

Barnumenthe & Baileys

1 oz. Baileys Irish cream
¼ oz. Hiram Walker white crème de menthe

Build.

Bart Simpson

½ oz. Malibu rum
½ oz. Midori melon liqueur
½ oz. Smirnoff vodka

Shake with ice, and strain into a shot glass.

Bart Simpson #2

¾ oz. Malibu Rum
¾ oz. Hiram Walker amaretto
¾ oz. Hiram Walker crème de banana
¼ oz. cream

Layer into a shot glass in the order given. Float cream on top.

Bartender on the Beach at Sunset

2 oz. pineapple juice
1 ¼ oz. Finlandia cranberry vodka
¼ oz. Chambord
¼ oz. Midori melon liqueur

Shake with ice, and strain into a shot glass.

Bazooka Shooter

1 oz. Southern Comfort
½ oz. crème de banana
Dash grenadine
Splash half-and-half

Shake with ice, and strain into a shot glass.

B.C.

1 part Absolut Citron vodka
1 part Kahlúa

Build.

B-Day

½ oz. Grand Marnier
½ oz. half-and-half
½ oz. Hiram Walker amaretto
½ oz. Kahlúa

Shake with ice, and strain into a shot glass.

Beach Ball

½ oz. blueberry schnapps
½ oz. Malibu rum
½ oz. pineapple juice

Shake with ice, and strain into a shot glass.

Beach Bum

¾ oz. Finlandia vodka
¾ oz. Midori melon liqueur
½ oz. cranberry juice

Shake with ice, and strain into a shot glass.

Beached Whale

1 oz. advocaat
½ oz. Cointreau
½ oz. white crème de cacao

Beam Me Up Scotty

½ oz. Kahlúa
½ oz. crème de banana
½ oz. Baileys Irish cream

Build.

Bear Hug

½ oz. Kahlúa
½ oz. Romana sambuca
½ oz. Grand Marnier

Build.

Beauty and the Beast

1 oz. Jägermeister, chilled
1 oz. Tequila Rose, chilled

 KEVIN WORTH • GOSHEN, NY

Beef on the Beach

1 oz. Beefeater gin
½ oz. cranberry juice
½ oz. peach schnapps
½ oz. pineapple juice

 JOE GARZA JR. • FRESNO, CA

Beer and Schöenauer

1 ½ oz. Schöenauer Apfel schnapps, chilled

Serve in a shot glass with your favorite beer on the side.

Beetlejuice

½ oz. amaretto
½ oz. cranberry juice
½ oz. Midori melon liqueur
½ oz. vodka

Bend Me Over

1 oz. Hiram Walker amaretto
¾ oz. pineapple juice
¼ oz. sweet and sour mix

Shake with ice, and strain into a shot glass.

Bengali Driving School

1 ½ oz. Midori melon liqueur
⅛ oz. Stolichnaya Razberi vodka
Splash Rose's lime juice
Maraschino cherry, stem removed

Mix first three ingredients in a tumbler and strain into the shot glass. Place the cherry in a shot glass. Viewed from above, the shooter resembles the Bangladesh national flag.

 CHRIS WERTZ • NEW YORK, NY

Berry Bad Juicer

1 part 99 Blackberries schnapps
1 part cranberry juice

Berry Berry

½ oz. Chambord
½ oz. cherry brandy
½ oz. orange juice

Shake with ice, and strain into a shot glass.

Berry Goldwater

1 oz. Der Lachs Original Danziger goldwasser
1 ½ oz. Echte Kroatzbeere blackberry liqueur

Build.

Berry Kix

4 oz. cranberry juice
1 ¼ oz. Absolut Kurant vodka
¼ oz. sweet and sour mix

Shake with ice, and strain into a shot glass.

Berry Nuts

½ oz. Frangelico
½ oz. Disaronno amaretto
½ oz. Chambord
½ oz. Baileys Irish cream

Build.

 MARY BELLMER • FENDERS—TURF INN • ALBANY, NY

Berry Patch

½ oz. blueberry schnapps
½ oz. raspberry schnapps
½ oz. strawberry schnapps
Splash orange juice

Shake with ice, and strain into a shot glass.

Between the Sheets

2 parts sweet and sour mix
1 part Bacardi rum
1 part brandy
1 part Cointreau

Shake with ice, and strain into a shot glass.

Big F Shooter

1 part Sambuca Molinari anisette liqueur
1 part peppermint schnapps
2 parts Bacardi 151 rum

Build.

Big Mo Shooter

1 part Absolut vodka
1 part Baileys Irish cream
1 part dark crème de cacao
1 part Disaronno amaretto
1 part Frangelico
1 part Kahlúa

Shake with ice, and strain into a shot glass.

Bikini

¾ oz. strawberry schnapps
¾ oz. Grand Marnier
¾ oz. vodka

Build.

Bikini Line

½ oz. Chambord
½ oz. Tia Maria
½ oz. vodka
Splash pineapple juice

Shake with ice, and strain into a shot glass.

Billy Blue Balls

¾ oz. peach schnapps
¾ oz. Stolichnaya Razberi vodka
¼ oz. blue curaçao
¼ oz. pineapple juice
Splash 7-Up
Splash sweet and sour mix

Mix and strain into shot glass.

 BILL GILLOTT • CLYDES AND COSTELLO'S •
TALLAHASSEE, FL

Bitch Bomb

1 oz. Killepitsch herbal liqueur
3 oz. of your favorite energy drink

Fill a shot glass with Killepitsch and then drop
into a 3-oz. glass of your favorite energy drink.

Bitch Slap

1 shot Fernet Branca Menta
Beer of your choice, for chaser

Bite the Bullet

¾ oz. Goldschläger
¾ oz. tequila
Splash Tabasco

B.J. Shooter

⅓ oz. Baileys Irish cream
⅓ oz. Grand Marnier

Build.

Black and Blue

1 oz. Romana sambuca
¾ oz. Kahlúa

 GEORGE P. GINTOLI • BRIDGEPORT, CT

Black Banana

¾ oz. Kahlúa
¾ oz. Hiram Walker crème de banana
¾ oz. Frïs vodka

Build.

Black Betty

1 oz. B&B liqueur
1 oz. Jägermeister

Shake with ice, and strain into a shot glass.

 TIM GALLAN • INDIANAPOLIS, IN

Black Blitzer

½ oz. Black Haus blackberry schnapps
½ oz. lemon juice
¼ oz. cranberry juice

Shake with ice, and strain into a shot glass.

 MARYBETH & BECKY HILL • WEST CHESTER, OH

Black Bull

¾ oz. Kahlúa
¾ oz. tequila

Shake with ice, and strain into a shot glass.

Black Cat

½ oz. Kahlúa
½ oz. apricot brandy
½ oz. ouzo

Build.

Black Death

½ oz. Bacardi 151 rum
½ oz. Kahlúa
½ oz. Romana sambuca
½ oz. Southern Comfort

Build.

 KEVIN CHURCH • LAS VEGAS CUE CLUB •
LAS VEGAS, NV

Black Devil Shooter

1 ½ oz. crème de menthe
1 oz. dark rum

Black Eye

⅓ oz. blackberry schnapps
⅓ oz. Rose's lime juice
⅓ oz. vodka

Shake with ice, and strain into a shot glass.

Black Forest

1 oz. Wild Turkey bourbon
½ oz. blackberry brandy

Shake with ice, and strain into a shot glass.

Black Ginger

⅔ oz. blackberry brandy
⅓ oz. ginger brandy

Serve straight up in a shot glass.

 TAMARA SLICHTA • BEBE'S PLACE • SLOAN, NY

Black Gold

¾ oz. Goldschläger, chilled
½ oz. Romana Black sambuca

Pour sambuca into ice-cold Goldschläger.

Black Jack Schlack

1 oz. Midori melon liqueur
1 oz. Myers's Original dark rum
Splash cola

Shake first two ingredients with ice and strain into a shot glass. Top with cola.

Black Jelly Bean

1 ½ oz. Chambord
Romana sambuca to float

Add Chambord to a shot glass. Float sambuca on top.

Black Mass

½ oz. Kahlúa
½ oz. Romana sambuca
½ oz. Bacardi 151 rum

Build.

Black Pearl

1 oz. Hiram Walker peach schnapps
½ oz. Hiram Walker blackberry brandy

Shake with ice, and strain into a shot glass.

Black Peppar

1 ¼ oz. Absolut Peppar vodka
¼ oz. Hiram Walker blackberry brandy

Shake with ice, and strain into a shot glass.

Black Rose

½ oz. blackberry brandy
¼ oz. Tequila Rose

Pour ingredients into a shot glass and serve.

 R. AMATO • BASKING RIDGE, NJ

Black Tie

2 parts Kahlúa
1 part Opal Nera black sambuca

Shake with ice, and strain into a shot glass.

Blackberry Cobbler

¾ oz. 99 Blackberries schnapps
¾ oz. Goldschläger
½ oz. cream

Chill and serve as a shooter.

Black-Eyed Susan

1 oz. Absolut Citron vodka
¼ oz. orange juice
¼ oz. pineapple juice

Shake with ice, and strain into a shot glass.

Black-Out

¾ oz. blackberry brandy
¾ oz. Tanqueray gin
⅛ oz. Rose's lime juice

Shake with ice, and strain into a shot glass.

Bleeding Heart

1 ¼ oz. Finlandia cranberry vodka
½ oz. Baileys Irish cream

Shake with ice, and strain into a shot glass.

Blitzkrieg Shooter

1 ½ oz. Rumple Minze peppermint
    schnapps
Splash Bacardi 151 rum

Serve chilled.

Blondie in Blue

2 ¼ oz. Blue Ice American vodka
⅓ oz. Marie Brizard Parfait Amour liqueur
¼ oz. Lillet Blonde
Lemon slice for garnish

Stir the ingredients in a mixing jar until they
are well chilled. Strain into a pre-chilled cocktail
glass and garnish with the lemon slice.

 JIMMY DOUGLAS • NEWPORT, VT

Blood Clot Shooter

1 ½ oz. Bacardi 151 rum
Dash grenadine
Half-and-half to float

Blood Rush

1 ½ oz. cherry brandy
1 oz. vodka

Build.

Bloody Brain

1 ½ oz. Baileys Irish cream
1 ½ oz. strawberry schnapps
Dash grenadine

Shake with ice, and strain into a shot glass.

Bloody Caesar

1 littleneck clam
2 drops Worcestershire sauce
2 drops Tabasco
Dash horseradish
1 oz. Frïs vodka
½ oz. tomato juice
Dash celery salt
Small lime wedge for garnish

Put the clam in the bottom of the shot glass. Add
Worcestershire sauce, Tabasco, and horseradish.
Add vodka and tomato juice. Sprinkle celery salt
and garnish with the small lime wedge.

Bloody Russian

1 part Absolut Peppar vodka
1 part cocktail sauce

Fill shooter halfway with cocktail sauce, then the
rest with vodka.

 GREG MAY • LIVERMORE, CA

Blooper

1 part 99 Grapes schnapps
1 part blue curaçao

Blow Job

1 part Baileys Irish cream
1 part Disaronno amaretto or Frangelico
1 part Kahlúa
Whipped cream to top

Shake with ice, and strain into a shot glass. Top
with whipped cream.

Blow Job #2

½ oz. Kahlúa
½ oz. Baileys Irish cream
½ oz. Absolut vodka
Whipped cream to top

Build. Top with whipped cream. Shoot without using hands by wrapping your lips around the glass and throwing your head back.

Blue Angel

1 oz. Hiram Walker blue curaçao
1 oz. orange juice

Shake with ice, and strain into a shot glass.

Blue Bayou

½ oz. blue curaçao
½ oz. Licor 43
½ oz. pineapple juice

Shake with ice, and strain into a shot glass.

Blue Bayou #2

¾ oz. blue curaçao
¾ oz. pineapple juice
¾ oz. Southern Comfort

 SHANE KARLIN • CAMPBELL, CA

Blue Bombay

1 oz. Bombay Sapphire gin
¼ oz. blue curaçao

Shake with ice, and strain into a shot glass.

Blue Carnation

¾ oz. cream
½ oz. blue curaçao
½ oz. white crème de menthe

Shake with ice, and strain into a shot glass.

Blue Flame

1 oz. Galliano
¼ oz. Bacardi 151 rum

Build.

Blue Fox

1 oz. blue curaçao
1 oz. Southern Comfort

Build.

Blue Hawaiian

¾ oz. Malibu rum
¼ oz. blue curaçao
¼ oz. orange juice
¼ oz. pineapple juice
¼ oz. white crème de cacao

Shake with ice, and strain into a shot glass.

Blue Ice

1 oz. vodka
¾ oz. sweet and sour mix
⅛ oz. blue curaçao
Splash Rose's lime juice

Shake with ice, and strain into a shot glass.

 ALI • SKI BAR • NEW YORK, NY

Blue Kamakazi

1 ½ oz. Finlandia vodka
⅛ oz. blue curaçao
Splash Rose's lime juice

Shake with ice, and strain into a shot glass.

Blue Lemonade

1 oz. Absolut Citron
¼ oz. blue curaçao
¼ oz. sweet and sour mix

Shake with ice, and strain into a shot glass.

Blue Marlin

1 oz. Bacardi rum
1 oz. lime juice
½ oz. blue curaçao

Stir with ice, and strain into a shot glass.

Blue Meanie

1 ½ oz. Sobieski vodka
¼ oz. blue curaçao
¼ oz. sweet and sour mix

Shake with ice, and strain into a shot glass.

 LAUREN SACCONE • ZOMBIE LOUNGE •
BASKING RIDGE, NJ

Blue Mojito

½ oz. club soda
½ oz. lime juice
½ oz. Stolichnaya Blueberi vodka
Splash peppermint schnapps
Splash simple syrup

Shake it up, strain, and shoot it down.

 MARK MCKEEVER • GRUMPY'S BAR •
MINNEAPOLIS, MN

Blue Monday

1 oz. vodka
¼ oz. Grand Marnier
1 dash blue curaçao

Shake with ice, and strain into a shot glass.

Blue Moon

1 ½ oz. blueberry schnapps
Dash blue curaçao
Dash sweet and sour mix

Shake the first two ingredients with ice and strain into a shot glass. Top with sweet and sour mix.

Blue Moon #2

½ oz. champagne
½ oz. blue curaçao
½ oz. orange juice

Build.

Blue Motorcycle

½ oz. Bacardi rum
½ oz. Beefeater gin
¼ oz. Frïs vodka
¼ oz. Hiram Walker blue curaçao
Dash sweet and sour mix
Dash ginger ale

Shake the first five ingredients with ice and strain into a shot glass. Top with ginger ale.

Blue Oil Slick

1 oz. Frïs vodka
½ oz. Hiram Walker blue curaçao
½ oz. Tia Maria

Shake with ice, and strain into a shot glass.

Blue Popper

1 oz. Hiram Walker blue curaçao
¾ oz. tequila
Splash Tabasco

Shake with ice, and strain into a shot glass.

Blue Skyy Kamikaze

1 oz. blue curaçao
1 oz. Skyy Infusions Citrus vodka
Splash Rose's lime juice

Chill, strain, and pour into a shot glass.

 BONNIE MCKESSON • BOAR'S HEAD SALOON •
JULIAN, CA

Blue Whale

¾ oz. peach schnapps
½ oz. blue curaçao
Dash sweet and sour mix
Dash club soda

Shake the first three ingredients with ice and
strain into a shot glass. Top with club soda.

Blue Whale #2

¾ oz. Myers's Original dark rum
¾ oz. blue curaçao
½ oz. pineapple juice

Build.

Bluebeard

½ oz. blueberry schnapps
1 ½ oz. vodka

Build.

Blueberry Cheesecake

½ oz. blueberry schnapps
½ oz. Disaronno amaretto
½ oz. Baileys Irish cream

Build.

Blueberry Hill

1 oz. milk or half-and-half
1 oz. vodka
½ oz. blue curaçao

Shake, strain, and shoot.

 PHILIP DEAN • LARRY'S DOCKSIDE GRILLE •
LAKE MARTIN, AL

Blueberry Lemonade

½ oz. blueberry schnapps
½ oz. vodka
¼ oz. cranberry juice
¼ oz. sweet and sour mix

Shake with ice, and strain into a shot glass.

Bluesberry

1 oz. half-and-half
¾ oz. blue curaçao
¾ oz. Chambord

Shake with ice, and strain into a shot glass.

Blushing Bride

1 part peach schnapps
1 part wildberry schnapps
1 part cranberry juice
1 part 7-Up

Build.

 WALKER & LINDA CALVERT • CALVERT'S INN •
LIVINGSTON, WI

Blushin' Russian Shooter

1 oz. Kahlúa
1 oz. Stolichnaya vodka
¼ oz. half-and-half
Disaronno amaretto to float

Shake the first three ingredients with ice and strain into a shot glass. Float Disaronno amaretto on top.

Bob Marley

1 part peppermint schnapps
1 part Myers's Original dark rum

Build.

Bocci Ball

¾ oz. Disaronno amaretto
¾ oz. Stolichnaya vodka
½ oz. orange juice

Shake with ice, and strain into a shot glass.

Bollweevil

½ oz. blackberry brandy
½ oz. Old Grand Dad bourbon
½ oz. Southern Comfort

Shake with ice, and strain into a shot glass.

Bomber Shooter

⅓ oz. Absolut vodka
⅓ oz. Disaronno amaretto
2 splashes pineapple juice

Shake with ice, and strain into a shot glass.

Bong Water

1 part amaretto
1 part Chambord
1 part Midori melon liqueur
1 part Southern Comfort
Splash Coke
Splash pineapple juice
Splash Sprite

 AL JACOBSON • TAYLORS ISLAND, MD

Bonzai Pipeline

1 oz. tropical fruit schnapps
½ oz. Absolut vodka

Stir with ice, and strain into a shot glass.

Booger

1 oz. Frïs vodka
½ oz. Malibu rum
½ oz. Midori melon liqueur
Splash pineapple juice

Shake with ice, and strain into a shot glass.

Boomer Shooter

¾ oz. apricot brandy
¾ oz. Monte Alban tequila
½ splash orange juice
½ splash sweet and sour mix

Shake with ice, and strain into a shot glass.

Border Conflict Shooter

¾ oz. Rumple Minze peppermint schnapps
¾ oz. Stolichnaya vodka
Splash grenadine

Stir and strain into a shot glass.

Bourbon Street

¾ oz. bourbon
¾ oz. Disaronno amaretto

Build.

Boxer Shorts

1 oz. Finlandia vodka
1 oz. Rumple Minze peppermint schnapps

Build.

Brain

¾ oz. Carolans Irish cream
½ oz. Hiram Walker peach schnapps
½ oz. Hiram Walker strawberry schnapps

Build.

Brain #2

1 oz. Southern Comfort
⅓ oz. Baileys Irish cream
⅓ oz. Cointreau

Shake with ice, and strain into a shot glass.

Brain Fart

½ oz. peach schnapps
Dash Kahlúa
Dash Crown Royal
2 dashes grenadine
½ oz. Baileys Irish cream

Add first four ingredients to a shot glass. Float
Baileys on top.

 JOSH WALTER • NAMPA, ID

Brain Hemorrhage

¾ oz. peach schnapps
½ oz. Baileys Irish cream
Drop grenadine

Build first two ingredients. Add grenadine in the
center.

Brain Teaser

⅓ oz. amaretto
⅓ oz. Baileys Irish cream
⅓ oz. sloe gin

Brandy Brainfreeze

1 ½ oz. E&J brandy
¾ cup strawberry daiquiri mix
Splash cherry brandy

Blend first two ingredients with ½ cup ice. Top
with cherry brandy. Serve in shot glasses.

 RORY L. CHATMAN • NORFOLK, VA

Brave Bull

1 part Jose Cuervo tequila
1 part Kahlúa

Build.

Brigantine Greenhead

1 oz. Absolut vodka
1 oz. Southern Comfort
1 oz. tequila
Splash green crème de menthe (just to color)

 GARY R. TRACY SR. • BRIGANTINE, NJ

Brighton Beach Hot Dog

1 ½ oz. Stolichnaya Peachnik vodka
8 oz. Red Dog beer

Pour vodka into a shot glass. Pour Red Dog into
an 8-oz. beer glass, and drop the shot glass into
the beer.

Bring the Pain

1 oz. Grande Absente absinthe
1 oz. Rumple Minze peppermint schnapps

Fill shot glass.

 LINDA VIETRO • BRONX, NY

Broken Leg

¾ oz. Canadian Club whisky
¾ oz. Hiram Walker peppermint schnapps

Shake with ice, and strain into a shot glass.

Brown Cow

1 oz. dark crème de cacao
¾ oz. Cointreau
¼ oz. half-and-half

Shake with ice, and strain into a shot glass.

Brown Cow #2

¾ oz. dark crème de cacao
¾ oz. white crème de cacao
½ oz. half-and-half

Shake with ice, and strain into a shot glass.

Brown Squirrel

½ oz. Hiram Walker amaretto
½ oz. Hiram Walker dark crème de cacao
¼ oz. half-and-half

Shake with ice, and strain into a shot glass.

Bubble Gum

½ oz. Frïs vodka
½ oz. Hiram Walker crème de banana
½ oz. Midori melon liqueur
½ oz. orange juice

Shake with ice, and strain into a shot glass.

Bubble Gum #2

1 oz. Finlandia cranberry vodka
1 oz. orange juice
¼ oz. crème de banana
¼ oz. peach schnapps

Shake with ice, and strain into a shot glass.

Bubble Gum #3

1 oz. orange juice
¾ oz. vodka
¼ oz. banana liqueur
¼ oz. peach schnapps

Shake with ice, and strain into a shot glass.

Bubble Gum #4

½ oz. crème de banana
½ oz. Midori melon liqueur
¼ oz. grenadine
¼ oz. orange juice
¼ oz. sweet and sour mix
¼ oz. vodka

Shake with ice, and strain into a shot glass.

Bubble Gum #5

¾ oz. blackberry brandy
¾ oz. Southern Comfort
¼ oz. half-and-half
⅛ oz. grenadine

Shake with ice, and strain into a shot glass.

Bucking Bronco

1 oz. Southern Comfort
½ oz. tequila

Build.

Buffalo Sweat

1 ½ oz. bourbon
Dash Tabasco

Pour bourbon into a shot glass. Add Tabasco.

Bull's Breath

1 part cranberry juice
1 part tequila
Splash Tabasco

 ANNE WILSON • WALL, NJ

Burning Bush Shooter

1 shot Monte Alban tequila
1 dash Tabasco

Build.

Bushwacker

1 oz. Baileys Irish cream
1 oz. Jameson Irish whiskey

Build.

Busted Cherry

½ oz. Kahlúa
½ oz. cherry brandy
½ oz. half-and-half

Build.

Butter Barrel Shooters

1 oz. A&W root beer
1 oz. DeKuyper Buttershots schnapps
1 oz. DeKuyper root beer schnapps

 ANGIE STOCKTON • HARTFORD, MI

Butterball

¾ oz. butterscotch schnapps
½ oz. Grand Marnier

Build.

Butterfly

1 part Carolans Irish cream
1 part Hiram Walker butterscotch schnapps

Build.

Butterscotch Slide

2 oz. milk
1 oz. Baileys Irish cream
1 oz. butterscotch schnapps
1 oz. Kahlúa

 DAVID TOTHILL • LOCKPORT, NY

Buttery Jäger Ripple

1 part Baileys Irish cream
1 part butterscotch schnapps
1 part Jägermeister

Shake with ice, and strain into a shot glass.

Buttery Nipple

¾ oz. butterscotch schnapps
¾ oz. Baileys Irish cream

Build.

Butt-Kicker

¾ oz. Chambord
¾ oz. Malibu rum
½ oz. Smirnoff vodka
Splash pineapple juice

 WAYNE SPARKS & JEAN MARIE PIETRO •
CARNEY'S PT., NJ

Buzzard's Breath

½ oz. Disaronno amaretto
½ oz. Kahlúa
½ oz. Rumple Minze peppermint schnapps

Stir with ice, and strain into a shot glass.

B.V.B.

½ oz. butterscotch schnapps
½ oz. Absolut vodka
½ oz. Baileys Irish cream

Float Absolut and Baileys over butterscotch schnapps.

 JIMMY OPPEL • BOBBY VALENTINE'S SPORTS
GALLERY CAFÉ • MIDDLETOWN, RI

Ca-Ca

¼ oz. amaretto
¼ oz. anisette
¼ oz. cherry brandy
¼ oz. Kahlúa

Shake with ice, and strain into a shot glass.

Cactus Blue

½ oz. DeKuyper cactus juice liqueur
½ oz. DeKuyper blue curaçao

Build.

Cactus Fever

1 ½ oz. DeKuyper cactus juice liqueur
Salt to taste
Lime juice to taste

Pour cactus juice liqueur into a shot glass. Add salt and lime to taste.

California Apple

1 oz. Bacardi Silver rum
½ oz. DeKuyper Sour Apple Pucker schnapps
½ oz. Peach schnapps
Splash cranberry juice

Shake with ice, and strain into a shot glass.

 ZAC CHICK • EL TORITO • CITRUS HEIGHTS, CA

California Kazi

¾ oz. vodka
¼ oz. Cointreau
¼ oz. Grand Marnier
¼ oz. Rose's lime juice

Shake with ice, and strain into a shot glass.

California Root Beer Shooter

1 oz. Kahlúa
½ oz. Galliano
Cola to top

Shake first two ingredients with ice and strain into a shot glass. Top with cola.

California Shot

¾ oz. Baileys Irish cream
¾ oz. Jose Cuervo Gold tequila
Splash coffee

Build.

 SAM THE SURFER • SANTA MONICA, CA

California Sizzler

1 part brandy
2 parts Malibu rum
2 parts orange juice

Build.

Canadian Boot

1 ½ oz. Yukon Jack whiskey
½ oz. Disaronno amaretto

 CRAIG ANGEL • UPLAND, CA

Candy Apple

¾ oz. Hiram Walker apple schnapps
¾ oz. Hiram Walker cinnamon schnapps
½ oz. cranberry juice

Shake with ice, and strain into a shot glass.

Candy Ass

¾ oz. Chambord
¾ oz. Mozart chocolate liqueur

Shake with ice, and strain into a shot glass.

Candy Cane

1 oz. Hiram Walker cherry-flavored brandy
1 oz. Hiram Walker peppermint schnapps

Shake with ice, and strain into a shot glass.

Cantaloupe

½ oz. Licor 43
½ oz. orange juice
½ oz. strawberry brandy

Shake with ice, and strain into a shot glass.

Cape Cod Shooter

1 oz. vodka
½ oz. cranberry juice

Shake with ice, and strain into a shot glass.

Capri

¾ oz. crème de banana
¾ oz. light cream
¾ oz. white crème de cacao

Shake with ice, and strain into a cordial glass.

Capt. Cotton Candy

1 oz. Captain Morgan Silver rum
1 oz. collins mix
½ oz. cranberry juice

 JASPER CAMPAGNA • SAN MATEO, CA

Capt. Kookaburra

1 oz. Captain Morgan rum
¾ oz. Baileys Irish cream

Pour Captain Morgan into a shot glass. Float
Baileys on top.

Captain on Acid

1 oz. Captain Morgan rum
½ oz. Midori melon liqueur
½ oz. pineapple juice
Splash sweet and sour mix

Shake over ice and strain into a shot glass.

 DALLAS BOLEN • DOG & DUCK PUB •
SUMMERVILLE, SC

Captain's Cannonball

2 parts orange juice
1 part Captain Morgan rum
1 part cranberry juice

Captain's Cream Soda Slammer

1 part Captain Morgan rum
1 part lemon-lime soda

Pour rum into a shot glass. Top with soda. Cover glass with a napkin. Slam down hard on a counter; serve immediately.

Captain's Hook

1 part Captain Morgan Parrot Bay rum
1 part Captain Morgan rum
1 part orange juice
1 part pineapple juice
Splash cranberry juice

 BARRY COLLINS • BUFFALO, NY

Caramel Apple

1 caramel candy
Schöenauer Apfel schnapps to fill

Put candy in a shot glass and fill with schnapps. Shoot the drink and chew the candy!

Caribbean Cruise Shooter

⅓ shot Kahlúa
⅓ shot Baileys Irish cream
⅓ shot CocoRibe coconut rum

Build.

Caribbean Quartet

3 parts pineapple juice
2 parts Midori melon liqueur
1 part Bacardi rum
1 part Captain Morgan rum
1 part Myers's Original dark rum
Splash grenadine

Shake with ice, and strain into a shot glass.

 KEITH MYERS • ITALIAN BISTRO • NEWARK, DE

Carnival Apple

1 oz. 99 Apples schnapps
½ oz. amaretto
½ oz. butterscotch schnapps

Shake with ice, and strain into a shot glass.

Carrot Cake Shooter

1 ½ oz. Baileys Irish cream
1 oz. DeKuyper Buttershots schnapps
½ oz. DeKuyper Hot Damn! cinnamon
  schnapps

 JUSTIN CRACCHIOLA • JOHNSON CITY, TN

C.B.

1 ¼ oz. Finlandia cranberry vodka
¼ oz. blueberry schnapps
⅛ oz. Cointreau

Shake with ice, and strain into a shot glass.

Cement Mixer

¾ oz. Baileys Irish cream
¾ oz. Rose's lime juice

Build.

Chambeird

½ oz. Chambord
½ oz. vodka
¼ oz. orange juice
¼ oz. pineapple juice

Shake with ice, and strain into a shot glass.

Chambord Iceberg

4 parts Chambord
1 part Absolut vodka

Shake with ice, and strain into a shot glass.

Champagne Royal

¼ oz. Chambord
1 ¾ oz. champagne

Build.

Chaps Inhaler

1 oz. blackberry brandy, chilled
½ oz. Goldschläger, chilled
½ oz. Rumple Minze peppermint schnapps,
   chilled

Serve in a shot glass.

 DONALD P. NOEL JR. • CHAP'S STEAKHOUSE AND
NITE CLUB • EDGEWATER, FL

Charlie Chaplin

1 oz. apricot brandy
1 oz. lemon juice
1 oz. sloe gin

Shake with ice, and strain into a cordial glass.

Charlie's Angel

¾ oz. amaretto
¼ oz. half-and-half

Shake with ice, and strain into a shot glass.

Cheerleader

1 oz. Disaronno amaretto
½ oz. cranberry juice
Dash Rose's lime juice

Shake with ice, and strain into a shot glass.

Cheesecake

1 ½ oz. half-and-half
1 oz. blueberry schnapps
½ oz. Kahlúa

Shake with ice, and strain into a shot glass.

Cherry Bomb

½ oz. crème de banana
½ oz. Kahlúa
¼ oz. cherry brandy
¼ oz. Myers's rum cream

Cherry Bomb #2

1 oz. cherry brandy
⅓ oz. Bacardi 151 rum

Build.

Cherry Chill

1 part 99 Black Cherries schnapps
1 part white rum

Cherry Hooper

¼ oz. cherry brandy
1 oz. orange juice

Build.

Cherry Lifesaver

1 oz. sweet and sour mix
¾ oz. cherry brandy
¼ oz. banana liqueur

Shake with ice, and strain into a shot glass.

Chia Pet

1 part Midori melon liqueur
1 part tequila

 RYAN PETERS • LIBERTY CORNER, NJ

Chiclet

1 oz. Jose Cuervo tequila
½ oz. Cointreau
Splash Rose's lime juice
Splash sweet and sour mix

 BAJA CANTINA • PARK CITY, UT

Chilled Kurant

1 ½ oz. Absolut Kurant vodka, chilled
2 maraschino cherries rolled in sugar

Drop cherries into a shot glass filled with vodka.

China Beach

1 part Domaine de Canton ginger liqueur
½ part vodka
2 parts cranberry juice

Build.

China White

⅓ oz. Baileys Irish cream
⅓ oz. Domaine de Canton ginger liqueur
⅓ oz. white crème de cacao

Chinese Torture

4 parts Domaine de Canton ginger liqueur
1 part Bombay gin

Build.

Chinese Torture #2

1 part Domaine de Canton ginger liqueur
1 part Bacardi 151 rum

Build.

Chip Shot

¾ oz. Baileys Irish cream
¾ oz. Tuaca liqueur
Splash coffee

Build.

Chip Shot #2

½ oz. Baileys Irish cream
½ oz. cream
½ oz. Kahlúa

Chocolate Almond Pie

¾ oz. dark crème de cacao
¾ oz. Disaronno amaretto
½ oz. half-and-half

Shake with ice, and strain into a shot glass.

Chocolate Banana

½ oz. banana liqueur
½ oz. dark crème de cacao
½ oz. half-and-half

Shake with ice, and strain into a shot glass.

Chocolate Cream Peaches

½ oz. Kahlúa
½ oz. peach schnapps
½ oz. half-and-half

Build.

Chocolate Kangaroo

1 oz. Tia Maria
½ oz. half-and-half
½ oz. Hiram Walker dark crème de cacao

Shake with ice, and strain into a shot glass.

Chocolate Milk

3 parts half-and-half
2 parts Mozart chocolate liqueur

Shake with ice, and strain into a shot glass.

Chocolate Milk Shake

½ oz. dark crème de cacao
½ oz. Licor 43
½ oz. milk

Shake with ice, and strain into a shot glass.

Chocolate Monkey

1 ½ oz. crème de banana
½ oz. dark crème de cacao
½ oz. half-and-half

Shake with ice, and strain into a shot glass.

Chocolate Mounds

½ oz. half-and-half
½ oz. Kahlúa
½ oz. Malibu rum

Shake with ice, and strain into a shot glass.

Chocolate Orgasm

½ oz. Baileys Irish cream
½ oz. Disaronno amaretto
½ oz. Mozart chocolate liqueur
½ oz. cream (optional)

Shake with ice, and strain into a shot glass.

Chocolate Pucker

½ oz. Absolut vodka
½ oz. crème de banana
½ oz. lemonade
½ oz. white crème de cacao

Shake with ice, and strain into a shot glass.

 JOE CARTER • CHARLIE & BARNEY'S BAR & GRILL
• INDIANAPOLIS, IN

Chocolate Raspberry

1 oz. Chambord
½ oz. half-and-half
½ oz. Kahlúa

Shake with ice, and strain into a shot glass.

Chocolate Rattlesnake Shooter

⅔ oz. Kahlúa
⅓ oz. white crème de cacao
⅔ oz. Baileys Irish cream
⅓ oz. Rumple Minze peppermint schnapps

Build.

Chocolate-Covered Cherry

½ oz. Kahlúa
½ oz. Baileys Irish cream
⅓ oz. grenadine

Build.

Chocolate-Covered Cherry #2

1 oz. Absolut Kurant vodka
½ oz. Baileys Irish cream
½ oz. Kahlúa
Maraschino cherry

Serve with the cherry on the bottom.

Chocolate-Covered Cherry #3

1 part grenadine
2 parts Disaronno amaretto
2 parts Baileys Irish cream

First put the grenadine on the bottom, then layer
amaretto and Baileys on top.

Choc-O-Mint

1 part Godiva chocolate liqueur
1 part Rumple Minze peppermint schnapps

Chill over ice and strain into a shot glass.

 GEORGIE ATFIELD • THE LIBRARY BAR &
RESTAURANT • WOODCLIFF LAKE, NJ

Chopper Stopper

3 oz. Holland House Strawberry Daiquiri
   Margarita Mix
1 oz. piña colada mix
½ oz. Absolut vodka
½ oz. Bacardi rum
¼ oz. Midori melon liqueur
¼ oz. pineapple juice

Pour into four shot glasses. Refrigerate. Serve cold, not frozen.

 K.W. CHAMBERLAIN • ANDOVER, MA

Christmas Candy Cane

1 oz. peppermint schnapps
½ oz. Romana sambuca
½ oz. Stolichnaya Vanil vodka
¼ oz. grenadine

Shake the first three ingredients over ice and strain into a shot glass. Slowly add grenadine for a red layer at the bottom.

 THAD DAVIS • THE AMAZON BAR & GRILL • SHERMAN OAKS, CA

Christmas Mist

1 oz. Cointreau
½ oz. Rumple Minze peppermint schnapps

Shake with ice, and strain into a shot glass.

Cincinnati Bengals

1 part Black Haus blackberry schnapps
1 part Stolichnaya Ohranj vodka

 MARYBETH & BECK HILL • WEST CHESTER, OH

Cinnamon Mold

1 ½ oz. cinnamon schnapps
½ oz. half-and-half

Shake with ice, and strain into a shot glass.

Circus Peanut

½ oz. crème de banana
½ oz. vodka
Splash grenadine
Whipped cream to top

Chill and shake. Top with whipped cream and serve.

 DAVE WARREN • BILLY FROGG'S GRILL & BAR • OMAHA, NE

Citron My Face

1 part Absolut Citron vodka
1 part cranberry juice
1 part Malibu Rum
1 part pineapple juice
1 part sweet and sour mix

 MARK J. SHEEHAN • FAIRFAX, VA

Citrus Shooter

¾ oz. Absolut vodka
¼ oz. Cointreau
¼ oz. cranberry juice
¼ oz. orange juice
¼ oz. pineapple juice

Shake with ice, and strain into a shot glass.

Clay Pigeon

1 oz. apple juice
1 oz. vodka

Shake with ice, and strain into a shot glass.

Clementine

1 oz. cranberry juice
¾ oz. Absolut Mandrin vodka
½ oz. sweet and sour mix

Stir in a shaker with ice. Strain into a shot glass.

 STEPHANIE S. RUSSELL • VERO BEACH, FL

Cloud 9

1 oz. Metaxa ouzo
½ oz. blueberry schnapps

Build.

Cloudy Day

1 oz. pineapple juice
¼ oz. Chambord
¼ oz. Malibu rum
¼ oz. Midori melon liqueur
Dash cream

Shake with ice, and strain into a shot glass.

Cloudy Skies

1 oz. Bulldog gin
¼ oz. blue curaçao

Build.

Clueless

1 oz. 4 Orange vodka
½ oz. Cointreau
½ oz. cranberry juice
½ oz. orange juice

Shake with ice, and strain into a shot glass.

Coco Loco Shot

1 oz. Coco López cream of coconut
1 oz. tequila

 AXEL BERENES • SAN JOSE, CA

Coconut Bon-Bon

½ oz. coconut rum
¼ oz. dark crème de cacao
¼ oz. Disaronno amaretto
¼ oz. half-and-half
¼ oz. orange juice

Shake with ice, and strain into a shot glass.

Coffee Bean

¾ oz. Kahlúa
¾ oz. anisette
¼ oz. Southern Comfort

Build.

Cold Gold

1 ½ parts Der Lachs Original Danziger
   goldwasser, chilled

Serve with your favorite beer on the side.

Colorado M.F.

½ oz. Absolut vodka
½ oz. half-and-half
½ oz. Kahlúa
¼ oz. Bacardi 151 rum
Dash club soda

Shake the first four ingredients with ice and
strain into a shot glass. Top with soda.

Coma

⅓ oz. anisette
⅓ oz. crème de banana
⅓ oz. Kahlúa

Comfort Zone

½ oz. Disaronno amaretto
½ oz. pineapple juice
½ oz. Southern Comfort

Shake with ice, and strain into a shot glass.

Comfortable Woo

½ oz. Absolut vodka
½ oz. cranberry juice
½ oz. peach schnapps
½ oz. Southern Comfort

Chill and strain.

 LORI STEWART • FRIEND'S RESTAURANT & PUB •
LOWELL, MA

Confetti Drops

1 oz. Jose Cuervo Especial tequila
½ oz. Goldschläger

Serve chilled in a shot glass.

Cool Citron

1 oz. Absolut Citron vodka
½ oz. Hiram Walker white crème de menthe

Build.

Cool Mint Listerine

⅓ oz. blue curaçao
⅓ oz. peppermint schnapps
⅓ oz. vodka

 FLIN BRIAN • KAMLOOPS, BRITISH COLUMBIA,
CANADA

Cool Peppar

1 ¼ oz. Absolut Peppar vodka, chilled
Lime wedge

Pour freezer-cold vodka into a shot glass. Squeeze
the juice of the lime wedge into the glass.

Cool-Aid

1 oz. cranberry juice
½ oz. Disaronno amaretto
½ oz. Midori melon liqueur
Club soda to top

Shake the first three ingredients with ice and strain into a shot glass. Top with soda.

Cool-Aid #2

⅓ oz. Midori melon liqueur
⅓ oz. Disaronno amaretto
⅓ oz. pineapple juice

Build.

Cool-Aid #3

⅓ oz. Southern Comfort
⅓ oz. Disaronno amaretto
⅓ oz. cranberry juice

Build.

Cordless Screwdriver

1 ¾ oz. Absolut vodka
Orange wedge
Sugar to cover orange wedge

Chill the vodka and strain it into a shot glass.
Dip the orange wedge in sugar. Shoot the vodka
and bite the orange.

Cosmic Aphrodisiac

½ oz. Bacardi Limón rum
½ oz. peach schnapps
½ oz. strawberry schnapps
Splash sweet and sour mix

 FREND GONDERMANN • PALATINE, IL

Cosmic Milk

1 oz. Tequila Rose
½ oz. amaretto
½ oz. banana liqueur

 GORAN PEROVIC • AKRON, OH

Cosmos

1 ½ oz. Finlandia vodka
½ oz. lime juice

Shake with ice, and strain into a shot glass.

Cough Drop

1 ¼ oz. blackberry brandy
1 ¼ oz. Rumple Minze peppermint
  schnapps

Build.

Cough Drop #2

¾ oz. Chambord
¾ oz. Rumple Minze peppermint schnapps

Build.

Cowboy

1 ½ oz. whiskey
½ oz. half-and-half

Shake with ice, and strain into a shot glass.

Crab Apple

1 oz. Red Bull
1 oz. Smirnoff Green Apple vodka
½ oz. Rose's Green Apple Cocktail Infusions

Combine in a shaker with ice and strain into a shot glass. Set the other 3 oz. of Red Bull aside for your friends.

 PATRICK KENNEDY, GARTH SMITH • COMFORT SUITES CARLISLE • CARLISLE, PA

Cracker Jack

½ oz. amaretto
½ oz. Frangelico
Splash vodka

Pour the ingredients over ice, stir, and strain into a shot glass.

 SCOTT MCMURTRAY • BLUE HORSE PUB AT THE BLEU ROCK INN • WASHINGTON, VA

Cran-A-Kazi

1 ½ oz. vodka
¼ oz. Cointreau
¼ oz. cranberry juice
¼ oz. Rose's lime juice

Shake with ice, and strain into a shot glass.

Cran-Apple

1 oz. apple schnapps
1 oz. cranberry juice

Shake with ice, and strain into a shot glass.

Cream of Beef

1 ¼ oz. Carolans Irish cream
½ oz. Beefeater gin

Build.

Cream Soda

¾ oz. Captain Morgan rum
½ oz. ginger ale

Build.

Creamsicle

1 oz. half-and-half
½ oz. Cointreau
½ oz. Galliano

Shake with ice, and strain into a shot glass.

Creamsicle #2

¾ oz. Licor 43
½ oz. orange juice
¼ oz. half-and-half
¼ oz. white crème de cacao

Shake with ice, and strain into a shot glass.

Creamy Saintsation

¾ oz. Baileys Irish cream
¾ oz. Maui tropical schnapps
¾ oz. Midori melon liqueur

 HARVEY SHIRAN • SAN ANTONIO, TX

Creature from the Black Lagoon

1 part Jägermeister
1 part Romana Black sambuca

Shake with ice, and strain into a shot glass.

Cripple Creek

1 oz. orange juice
½ oz. Old Grand Dad bourbon
½ oz. tequila
¼ oz. Galliano

Shake the first three ingredients with ice and strain into a shot glass. Float Galliano on top.

Crispy Shooter

½ oz. Disaronno amaretto
½ oz. Kahlúa
¼ oz. Rumple Minze peppermint schnapps

Shake with ice, and strain into a shot glass.

Cross-Eyed Mary

¾ oz. Bacardi Limón rum
¾ oz. Beefeater gin
Splash cola

Shake with ice, and strain into a shot glass.

 BONNIE S. BAILEY • WAPPINGERS FALLS, NY

Cruise Missile

½ oz. blue curaçao
½ oz. crème de noyaux
¼ oz. grapefruit juice
¼ oz. vodka

Shake with ice, and strain into a shot glass.

Cuervo Popper

1 oz. Jose Cuervo Gold tequila
¼ oz. ginger ale

Build.

Curly Cue

1 part Baileys Irish cream
1 part Goldschläger

Shake with ice, and strain into a shot glass.

 MARY GIBBESON • DEER LODGE • OJAI, CA

Dallas Alice

1 part amaretto
1 part Grand Marnier
1 part tequila

Shake with ice, and strain into a shot glass.

Darlington's Delight

Green crème de menthe
Godet Belgian white chocolate liqueur

Pour crème de menthe into a shot glass. Layer
Godet liqueur on top.

 JIM DARLINGTON • ASTOR, PA

Day in the Shade

1 oz. Malibu Rum
½ oz. cranberry juice
½ oz. pineapple juice

Shake with ice, and strain into a shot glass.

DC-3

½ oz. anisette
⅓ oz. Baileys Irish cream
⅓ oz. Kahlúa

Dead Canary

1 oz. Finlandia vodka
¼ oz. Grand Marnier
¼ oz. pineapple juice

Shake with ice, and strain into a shot glass.

Dead Doctor

1 part Dr. McGillicuddy's Mentholmint
   schnapps
1 part Jägermeister
1 part Kahlúa

Serve chilled in shot glass.

 CINDY SMITH • BOB SMITH'S SPORTS CLUB •
HUDSON, WI

Dead Rat

1 oz. Usquaebach scotch whisky
⅓ oz. yellow Chartreuse

Shake with ice, and strain into a shot glass.

Death Wish

1 part Jägermeister
1 part Rumple Minze peppermint schnapps
1 part Wild Turkey bourbon

Mix and pour into shot glasses.

Debonair Shot

1 oz. scotch whiskey
¼ oz. Domaine de Canton ginger liqueur

Stir ingredients together with ice to chill. Shake and strain into a chilled shot glass.

 BILL MCCABE • FT. LAUDERDALE, FL

Deep Throat

½ oz. Frïs vodka
½ oz. Kahlúa
Whipped cream to top

Dennis the Menace

1 oz. Malibu rum
½ oz. peach schnapps
Splash cranberry juice

Shake with ice, and strain into a shot glass.

Depth Charge

1 mug beer
1 oz. Rumple Minze peppermint schnapps

Pour Rumple Minze into a shot glass. Drop the shot glass in the beer and down.

Desert Sunrise

1 oz. DeKuyper cactus juice liqueur
Splash Rose's lime juice

Serve chilled.

Designer Jeans

½ oz. Baileys Irish cream
½ oz. Chambord
½ oz. Myers's Original dark rum

Shake with ice, and strain into a shot glass.

Devil You Don't Know

1 part Jägermeister
1 part Mozart chocolate liqueur

Build.

Devil's Blood

1 ¼ oz. tequila
¾ oz. tomato juice
Splash Tabasco

Shake with ice, and strain into a shot glass.

Dew and a Brew

1 shot Tullamore Dew Irish whiskey
1 beer

Enjoy a shot with a beer.

Dezez Blueberry Blast

½ shot Frangelico
½ shot Stolichnaya Blueberi vodka
Splash of cranberry juice

Shake then pour into a shot glass.

 DESIREE MELENDEZ • HIBISCUS CLUB •
HONOLULU, HI

Dirty Adrian

½ oz. Baileys Irish cream
½ oz. Dr. McGillicuddy's vanilla schnapps
½ oz. Godiva chocolate liqueur

 JAMES BYRNE • OSWEGO, NY

Dirty Devil

¾ oz. vodka
½ oz. Kahlúa
½ oz. Galliano
Lime wheel
Dash sugar
Bacardi 151 rum to float

Layer the first three ingredients in order. Place the lime wheel over the shot glass, sprinkle with sugar. Float rum on the wheel.

Dirty Harry

1 oz. Grand Marnier
1 oz. Tia Maria

Shake with ice, and strain into a shot glass.

Dirty Leprechaun

1 part Jägermeister
1 part Baileys Irish cream
1 part Midori melon liqueur

Build or shake with ice.

Dirty Peach

¾ oz. peach schnapps
½ oz. half-and-half
½ oz. Kahlúa
Dash pineapple juice

Shake with ice, and strain into a shot glass.

Dog Breath

1 ½ oz. Fernet Branca
1 Red Dog beer

Shoot Fernet Branca with Red Dog on the side.

Dollar Bill

1 oz. Frïs vodka
¾ oz. Midori melon liqueur
⅛ oz. Rose's lime juice

Shake with ice, and strain into a shot glass.

Don

¼ oz. dark crème de cacao
¼ oz. white crème de cacao
¼ oz. gin
1 oz. vodka

Layer in a shot glass.

Don Q Cristal Kiss

4 oz. Tropicana orange juice
1 ½ oz. Don Q Cristal rum
½ oz. blue curaçao

Shake with ice, and strain into a shot glass.

Double Jack

½ oz. Jack Daniel's whiskey
½ oz. Yukon Jack whiskey

Shake with ice, and strain into a shot glass.

Double Vision

1 oz. Tia Maria
¼ oz. brandy
¼ oz. Romana sambuca

Shake with ice, and strain into a shot glass.

Doublemint

1 part Hiram Walker peppermint schnapps
1 part Hiram Walker spearmint schnapps

Build.

Dr. Pepper

1 part Disaronno amaretto
1 part root beer schnapps
⅔ oz. glass of beer

Fill a shot glass with amaretto and root beer schnapps. Drop the shot glass into the beer.

Drambuie Dragon

2 oz. Drambuie
6 drops Tabasco

Coat a shot glass with Tabasco, fill with Drambuie, and serve straight up.

Dream Shake

1 oz. Baileys Irish cream
½ oz. Tia Maria

Shake with ice, and strain into a shot glass.

Dreamsicle

1 ¼ oz. amaretto
½ oz. half-and-half
½ oz. orange juice

Shake with ice, and strain into a shot glass.

Drunk Irish Monk

1 ¼ oz. Carolans Irish cream
¾ oz. Hiram Walker hazelnut liqueur

Shake with ice, and strain into a shot glass.

Drunk Monk

1 ¼ oz. Bacardi rum
¾ oz. Hiram Walker hazelnut liqueur

Shake with ice, and strain into a shot glass.

Duck Fart

¾ oz. Kahlúa
¾ oz. Carolans Irish cream
½ oz. Canadian Club whisky

Build.

Duck Pin

¾ oz. Chambord
¾ oz. Stolichnaya vodka
½ oz. pineapple juice

Shake with ice, and strain into a shot glass.

Duck Pin #2

1 oz. Chambord
½ oz. pineapple juice
½ oz. Southern Comfort

Shake with ice, and strain into a shot glass.

Dunham Good

1 oz. Goldschläger
½ oz. Disaronno amaretto

Shake with ice, and strain into a shot glass.

Dunikaze

1 part amaretto
1 part blackberry brandy
1 part Rumple Minze peppermint schnapps
Jim Beam bourbon to float

Add the first three ingredients to a shot glass and float bourbon on top.

Dusty Rose

1 oz. Baileys Irish cream
1 oz. Chambord

Shake with ice, and strain into a shot glass.

Earthquake

¾ oz. anisette
¾ oz. Disaronno amaretto
¼ oz. Southern Comfort

Build.

Earthquake #2

1 part Disaronno amaretto
1 part Jim Beam After Shock

 LYNN KIRSCH • WINTER PARK, FL

Easter Egg

½ oz. Chambord
½ oz. Tia Maria
½ oz. half-and-half

Build.

Ejaculation

¾ oz. vodka
½ oz. Baileys Irish cream
½ oz. white crème de cacao
½ oz. white crème de menthe

 RAMSEY LUKE • BEVERLY HILLS, CA

E.K. Up

2 parts Echte Kroatzbeere blackberry
  liqueur

Serve straight up, well chilled.

El Chico

1 oz. tequila
½ oz. Cointreau
½ oz. Rose's lime juice
2 dashes Angostura bitters

Shake with ice, and strain into a shot glass.

El Torito

1 oz. Sauza Conmemorativo tequila
½ oz. Hiram Walker dark crème de cacao

Build.

Electric Banana

½ oz. tequila
½ oz. crème de banana

Build.

Electric Popsicle

½ oz. Chambord
½ oz. vodka
½ oz. crème de banana
½ oz. lime juice

Build.

Electric Sambuca

1 shot sambuca
1 shot blue curaçao

Build.

 DON VOIGHT • WILLOW SPRINGS, IL

Elephant's Foot

1 part Grand Marnier
1 part half-and-half
1 part Kahlúa
1 part Licor 43
1 part Stolichnaya vodka

Shake with ice, and strain into a shot glass.

Elwoods Shooter

1 oz. pineapple juice
¾ oz. amaretto
Dash crème de cassis

Shake with ice, and strain into a shot glass.

Empire Strikes Back

¼ oz. Disaronno amaretto
¼ oz. Grand Marnier
¼ oz. pineapple juice
¼ oz. Smirnoff 100 vodka
¼ oz. Southern Comfort

Shake with ice, and strain into a shot glass.

Energizer

½ oz. Benedictine
½ oz. Baileys Irish cream
½ oz. Grand Marnier

Build.

Environmintz

1 ½ oz. 360 vodka
½ oz. Rumple Minze peppermint schnapps
York peppermint pattie for garnish

Serve chilled. Garnish with the York peppermint
pattie.

 BILL BONA • CELEBRATION TOWN TAVERN •
CELEBRATION, FL

Equalizer

¾ oz. Jägermeister
½ oz. orange juice
½ oz. peach schnapps
½ oz. pineapple juice

Shake with ice, and strain into a shot glass.

Erin Cross

¾ oz. Baileys Irish cream
¾ oz. Celtic Crossing Irish liqueur
½ oz. Black Bush Irish whiskey

 MIKE BYERS • FIFE, WA

Eskimo Slugger

1 part Baileys Irish cream
1 part California butterscotch schnapps
1 part Rumple Minze peppermint schnapps

 CRAIG HAYEN • BROOKINGS, SD

E.T.

⅓ oz. Midori melon liqueur
½ oz. Baileys Irish cream
⅓ oz. Absolut vodka

Build.

Evening Shade

¾ oz. Baileys Irish cream
¾ oz. DeKuyper ButYou Buttershots schnapps
Splash pineapple juice

 PAM PAYTON • ST. ROBERTS, MO

Eye Drop

½ oz. Rumple Minze peppermint schnapps
½ oz. Metaxa ouzo
½ oz. Stolichnaya vodka

Build.

Eye to Eye (I to I)

1 oz. Carolans Irish cream
1 oz. Tullamore Dew Irish whiskey

Shake with ice, and strain into a shot glass.

F-16

1 part Kahlúa
1 part Baileys Irish cream
1 part brandy

Build.

F-16 #2

1 part Kahlúa
1 part Baileys Irish cream
1 part Bacardi 151 rum

Build.

F-16 #3

½ oz. Carolans Irish cream
½ oz. Hiram Walker hazelnut liqueur
½ oz. Kahlúa

Shake with ice, and strain into a shot glass.

F-52

1 part Kahlúa
1 part Baileys Irish cream
1 part Frangelico

Build.

Fanny Pack

2 oz. orange juice
1 oz. Finlandia vodka
½ oz. Finlandia cranberry vodka
¼ oz. pineapple juice

Shake with ice, and strain into a shot glass.

Fender Bender

1 part peach schnapps
1 part green Chartreuse

Build.

Fernet Brandy

1 oz. brandy
½ oz. Fernet Branca

Fifth Avenue

½ oz. dark crème de cacao
½ oz. apricot-flavored brandy
1 tbsp. light cream

Layer in order in a cordial glass.

Fifty-Fifty (50-50) Bar

1 oz. Baileys Irish cream
1 oz. Kahlúa
Splash Bacardi 151 rum

Add the first two ingredients to a shot glass.
Float rum on top.

Fifty-Seven ('57) T-Bird

½ oz. Disaronno amaretto
½ oz. Grand Marnier
½ oz. pineapple juice
½ oz. Southern Comfort

Shake with ice, and strain into a shot glass.

Fifty-Seven ('57) T-Bird with Detroit Plates

1 part amaretto
1 part Grand Marnier
1 part pineapple juice
1 part Southern Comfort
1 part vodka

Shake with ice, and strain into a shot glass.

Fifty-Seven ('57) T-Bird with Texas Plates

1 part Grand Marnier
1 part grapefruit juice
1 part Myers's Original dark rum
1 part sloe gin

Shake with ice, and strain into a shot glass.

Finger Wiggle

½ oz. Malibu rum
¼ oz. DeKuyper Crantasia schnapps
Splash Absolut Citron vodka
Splash cranberry juice
Splash sweet and sour mix

 CHRISTINE "CK" KOTILA • WARREN, MI

Finnigan's Wake

1 oz. Finlandia vodka
½ oz. pineapple juice
¼ oz. melon liqueur

Mix as a shot.

Fire & Ice

¾ oz. Rumple Minze peppermint schnapps
¾ oz. Bacardi 151 rum

Build.

Fire Bomb

¾ oz. Frïs vodka
¾ oz. Hiram Walker cinnamon schnapps
Dash cayenne pepper
Dash Tabasco

Shake with ice, and strain into a shot glass.

Fire in the Holt!

5 oz. ginger ale
1 shot Fireball Cinnamon Whisky

Fill a shot glass with whiskey, drop into ginger
ale, and drink the whole thing.

 ANDREW JORDAN • SEATTLE, WA

Fireball

1 oz. cherry brandy
1 oz. Dr. McGillicuddy's Mentholmint
   schnapps

Shake with ice, and strain into a shot glass.

Fireball #2

1 oz. cinnamon schnapps
½ oz. grenadine
½ oz. vodka

Shake with ice, and strain into a shot glass.

Fireball #3

1 ½ oz. cinnamon schnapps
Dash Tabasco

Shake with ice, and strain into a shot glass.

Fire-Breathing Dragon

1 part Bacardi 151 rum
1 part Goldschläger
2 drops Tabasco

 RORY L. CHATMAN • NORFOLK, VA

Firecracker

1 part blue curaçao
1 part Baileys Irish cream
1 part sloe gin

In a shooter glass, float the first two ingredients
to form layers. Pour sloe gin lightly on top.

 ALICE WHITMER • PELLES SPORTS BAR •
FAIR HAVEN, MI

Firecracker #2

¾ oz. Rumple Minze peppermint schnapps
Drop Tabasco
Dash grenadine
Dash club soda

Shake schnapps and Tabasco with ice and strain
into a shot glass. Dribble in grenadine and soda.

Firewater

1 part Rumple Minze peppermint schnapps
1 part cinnamon schnapps
3 drops Bacardi 151 rum

Build.

Flame

1 ¼ oz. Absolut Peppar vodka
¼ oz. Cherry Marnier

Build.

Flame Thrower

⅓ oz. white crème de cacao
⅓ oz. Benedictine
⅓ oz. brandy

Build.

Flaming Red Bush

1 oz. Dr. McGillicuddy's Mentholmint
   schnapps
1 oz. Red Bull

Put in a shot glass. Slam and drink.

 SHERLY ROOK • LANDO'S • CORNING, NY

Flaming Shorts

⅓ oz. Kahlúa
⅓ oz. Baileys Irish cream
⅓ oz. green Chartreuse

Build.

Floaters Shooter

1 oz. orange juice
½ shot Black Velvet Canadian whisky

Add orange juice to a shot glass and float whiskey on top.

Florida Joy

1 ¼ oz. Absolut Citron vodka
½ oz. Grand Marnier

Mix with cracked ice in a shaker or blender and pour into a shot glass.

Flu Shot

1 can Red Bull
½ oz. Skyy Infusions Citrus vodka
⅓ oz. blue curaçao
⅓ oz. Midori melon liqueur

Pour Red Bull into a glass. Shake and strain the next three ingredients into a shot glass and drop into the Red Bull.

 DARCY LARKIN • APPLEBEE'S/BROWNSBURG • INDIANAPOLIS, IN

Flying Banana

½ oz. Captain Morgan Parrot Bay rum
½ oz. crème de banana
½ oz. Orange juice
Splash grenadine

Shake with ice, and strain into a shot glass.

Flying Grasshopper

½ oz. green crème de menthe
½ oz. Smirnoff vodka
½ oz. white crème de cacao

Stir with ice, and strain into a cordial glass.

Flying Purple People Eater

1 part blue curaçao
1 part DeKuyper Berry Fusion Pucker
   schnapps
1 part Absolut vodka
Cranberry juice to fill

Build.

 JENNIFER LISA WEIR • AMERICAN ATHLETIC CLUB
CAFÉ • MILFORD, MA

Fog

1 oz. Stolichnaya vodka
½ oz. cranberry juice
Juice of fresh lime

Shake with ice, and strain into a shot glass.

Foghorn

¾ oz. Bombay gin
¾ oz. ginger ale
Dash Rose's lime juice

Shake with ice, and strain into a shot glass.

Fool's Gold

½ oz. Goldschläger
½ oz. Stolichnaya Vanil vodka

Shake and strain into a shot glass.

 ADAM E. • PHILADELPHIA, PA

Forbidden Cinnamon Apple

½ oz. Leroux apple schnapps
¼ oz. Absolut vodka
¼ oz. Goldschläger

Chill over ice and strain into a shooter glass.

 GEORGIE ATFIELD • THE LIBRARY BAR &
RESTAURANT • WOODCLIFF LAKE, NJ

Fortified

2 parts DeKuyper cactus juice liqueur
1 part Jose Cuervo Especial tequila

 DONNA LUTHER • KETCHIKAN, AK

Fourth of July

¾ oz. Rumple Minze peppermint schnapps
¾ oz. blue curaçao
Splash grenadine

Build.

Foxy Lady

1 oz. Disaronno amaretto
½ oz. Stolichnaya vodka
1 oz. blue curaçao

Layer in order in a cordial glass.

Frazzle

1 oz. Baileys Irish cream
1 oz. Captain Morgan rum

Build. Serve in a shot glass.

 SHARON MCHENRY • TOMMY'S MARDI GRAS •
STONE PARK, IL

Freddy Kruger

¼ oz. Romana sambuca
¼ oz. Jägermeister
¾ oz. vodka

Build.

French Choo Choo

1 oz. Grand Marnier
1 oz. Southern Comfort

Shake with ice, and strain into a shot glass.

French Connection

1 part Courvoisier cognac
1 part Grand Marnier

Shake with ice, and strain into a shot glass.

French Hooker

¾ oz. Absolut vodka
¾ oz. Chambord
Splash sweet and sour mix

Stir and strain into a shot glass.

French Kamikaze

¾ oz. vodka
½ oz. Chambord
Dash Rose's lime juice

Shake with ice, and strain into a shot glass.

French Kiss

1 part Martini & Rossi sweet vermouth
1 part Martini & Rossi dry vermouth

Build.

French Tickler

⅔ oz. Goldschläger
½ oz. Grand Marnier

Shake with ice, and strain into a shot glass.

French Toast

1 oz. cinnamon schnapps
1 oz. club soda

Build.

Frïs Your Nuts

½ oz. Frïs vodka
½ oz. Hiram Walker hazelnut liqueur

Shake with ice, and strain into a shot glass.

Fritzel's Half and Half

1 oz. Bismarck vodka
1 oz. Schöenauer Apfel schnapps

 MATTHEW TAG • NEW YORK, NY

Frog in a Blender

½ oz. Jägermeister
1 oz. Baileys Irish cream
½ oz. green crème de menthe
Grenadine to rim glass
Sugar to rim glass

Shake Jägermeister and Baileys with ice. Strain into a shot glass rimmed with grenadine and sugar. Add crème de menthe very slowly, drop by drop. It should look like a blended frog.

 MAX BURNETT • STUDIO CITY, CA

Fru-Fru

1 part banana liqueur
1 part peach schnapps
1 part pineapple juice
Splash lime juice

Build.

Fruit & Nuts

¾ oz. Chambord
¾ oz. Frangelico
½ oz. cranberry juice
¼ oz. half-and-half

 AMY JANE LOUISE • HOBOKEN, NJ

Fruit Lifesaver

¾ oz. Hiram Walker crème de banana
¾ oz. Hiram Walker blackberry brandy

Build.

Fruit Punch Tequila

1 shot tequila
Splash DeKuyper Island Punch Pucker
  schnapps

Full Moon

¾ oz. Grand Marnier
¾ oz. Hiram Walker amaretto liqueur

Build.

Funky Bitch

½ oz. Kahlúa
½ oz. vodka
¼ oz. Baileys Irish cream
¼ oz. Frangelico

Shake with ice, and strain into a shot glass.

Funky Monkey

¼ oz. Baileys Irish cream
¼ oz. butterscotch schnapps
¼ oz. crème de banana
¼ oz. half-and-half

 STEVE COCHRAN • IRVINE, CA

Fuzzy Antler

¾ oz. Canadian Mist whisky
¾ oz. peach schnapps

Shake with ice, and strain into a shot glass.

Fuzzy Melon

1 oz. Hiram Walker peach schnapps
1 oz. Midori melon liqueur
Splash half-and-half
Splash orange juice
Splash pineapple juice

Shake with ice, and strain into a shot glass.

Fuzzy Mexican

1 oz. Jose Cuervo 1800 tequila
Splash DeKuyper Peachtree schnapps

Build.

 ROBERT TURLINGTON • BROCKPORT, NY

Fuzzy Monkey

1 oz. crème de banana
¾ oz. orange juice
¼ oz. peach schnapps

Shake with ice, and strain into a shot glass.

 SCOTT SWIGART • EAST VILLAGE GRILL AND BAR
• RALEIGH, NC

Fuzzy Navel

1 part DeKuyper Peachtree schnapps
2 parts orange juice

Build.

Fuzzy Pirate

½ oz. Captain Morgan rum
½ oz. peach schnapps
1 oz. cranberry juice

Build.

G&C

⅓ oz. Galliano
⅔ oz. Rémy Martin cognac

Float cognac on Galliano in a 1-oz. pony glass.

G&G

1 oz. Galliano
½ oz. Candolini grappa

Build.

Galactic Ale

1 oz. blue curaçao
1 oz. Frïs vodka
1 oz. lime juice
½ oz. Chambord

Shake with ice, and strain into a shot glass.
Serves two.

Galliano Hot Shot

¾ oz. Galliano
¾ oz. hot coffee
Whipped cream to top

Put hot coffee into a shot glass. Add Galliano.
Top with whipped cream.

Galliano Viking

¾ oz. Galliano
¾ oz. vodka

Build.

Gallstone Shooter

¾ oz. crème de noyaux
¾ oz. white crème de cacao
½ oz. Absolut vodka

Shake and strain into a shot glass.

Gangrene

1 part Jägermeister
1 part Midori melon liqueur

Build.

Gargleblaster

½ oz. Midori melon liqueur
1 oz. Bacardi rum
¼ oz. Bacardi 151 rum

Build.

Garter Belt

1 ¼ oz. Bacardi Amber rum

Serve in shot glass.

Gator Hater

1 ½ oz. Absolut Mandrin, chilled
½ oz. blue curaçao, chilled
½ mug Red Bull

Strain first two ingredients into a shot glass.
Drop into the Red Bull.

 RUSSELL BRUKE • POCKETS POOL & PUB •
TALLAHASSEE, FL

Gator Juice

2 parts Southern Comfort
1 part blue curaçao
1 part orange juice
Splash Rose's lime juice

Shake with ice, and strain into a shot glass.

German Death

½ oz. Jägermeister
½ oz. Rumple Minze peppermint schnapps

Build.

German Milkshake

1 oz. dark crème de cacao
1 oz. half-and-half
1 oz. Jäagermeister

Shake with ice, and strain into a shot glass.

Ghostbusters

¾ oz. peach schnapps
¾ oz. vodka
Dash cranberry juice
Dash half-and-half
Dash orange juice

Shake and strain into a shot glass.

Gin & Sin

1 ½ oz. Beefeater gin
½ oz. orange juice
½ oz. sweet and sour mix
Splash grenadine

Shake with ice, and strain into a shot glass.

Ginger Snap

1 ½ oz. Domaine de Canton ginger liqueur
½ oz. sparkling water

Shoot.

Glow Work

¾ oz. Midori melon liqueur
¾ oz. Old Grand Dad bourbon
½ oz. pineapple juice

Shake and strain into a shot glass.

Godchild

¾ oz. Disaronno amaretto
¾ oz. brandy

Build.

Godfather

¼ oz. Disaronno amaretto
1 ¼ oz. J&B scotch whisky

Build.

Godmother

½ oz. Disaronno amaretto
1 ½ oz. Stolichnaya vodka

Build.

Gold Freeze

Keep a bottle of Der Lachs Original Danziger goldwasser in the freezer; enjoy ice shots straight up.

Gold Furnace

1 oz. Goldschläger
2 dashes Tabasco

Build.

Gold Rush

½ oz. Goldschläger
½ oz. Jose Cuervo Gold tequila

Build.

Gold Russian

1 part Goldschläger
1 part Kahlúa

Shake with ice, and strain into a shot glass.

Golden Apple

¾ oz. DeKuyper Sour Apple Pucker
   schnapps
¼ oz. Goldschläger

Layer Goldschläger on top of Sour Apple Pucker
schnapps.

 BRETT MAY • HUGHESVILLE, PA

Golden Cadillac

1 oz. half-and-half
½ oz. Galliano
½ oz. white crème de cacao

Shake with ice, and strain into a shot glass.

Golden Dragon

1 ¾ oz. brandy
1 tbsp. yellow Chartreuse

Pour Chartreuse into a shot glass and float
brandy on top.

Golden Dream

½ oz. Cointreau
½ oz. Galliano
½ oz. half-and-half
½ oz. orange juice

Shake with ice, and strain into a shot glass.

Golden Gorilla

½ oz. Hiram Walker crème de banana
½ oz. orange juice
½ oz. pineapple juice
½ oz. Puerto Rican rum
¼ oz. Galliano

Shake the first four ingredients with ice and strain into a shot glass. Float Galliano on top.

 JACK HOWLEY • TAMPA, FL

Golden Nipple

¾ oz. Galliano
¾ oz. Kahlúa
Whipped cream to top

Pour Galliano into a shooter glass, then carefully float Kahlúa on top. Top with whipped cream.

Golden Spike

¾ oz. Galliano
¾ oz. Drambuie
¼ oz. J&B scotch whisky

Build.

Goldfinger

1 ½ oz. Goldschläger, chilled

Serve and lick the finger!

Goldschläger & Lager

1 ½ oz. Goldschläger, chilled
12 oz. beer, chilled

Shoot ice-cold Goldschläger with an ice-cold beer.

Good & Plenty

¾ oz. Hiram Walker anisette
¾ oz. Kahlúa

Shake with ice, and strain into a shot glass.

Good & Plenty #2

1 oz. anisette
1 oz. blackbérry brandy

Build.

Good & Plenty #3

¼ oz. Frïs vodka
½ oz. half-and-half
¼ oz. Hiram Walker anisette
¼ oz. Kahlúa

Shake with ice, and strain into a shot glass.

Goodnight

1 part Avalanche peppermint schnapps
1 part Goldschläger
1 part Jim Beam After Shock

 RYAN CLARK • ORLANDO, FL

Gorilla Fart Shooter

1 part Bacardi 151 rum
1 part Wild Turkey bourbon

Build.

Graham Cracker

½ oz. Baileys Irish cream
½ oz. butterscotch schnapps
½ oz. Goldschläger
½ oz. half-and-half

Gran-Cran

1 oz. Finlandia cranberry vodka
¼ oz. Grand Marnier

Build.

Grand Am

1 part Grand Marnier
1 part Disaronno amaretto

Build.

Grand Slam

2 parts orange juice
2 parts Tanqueray gin
1 part Grand Marnier
Splash grenadine
Maraschino cherry for garnish

Shake with ice, pour into a test tube, and top it
off with a cherry.

Grape Ape

1 part Absolut vodka
2 parts grape juice
1 part 7-Up

Build.

Grape Crush

1 oz. Smirnoff vodka
½ oz. Chambord
½ oz. sweet and sour mix
7-Up to top

Shake the first three ingredients with ice and
strain into a shot glass. Top with 7-Up.

Grape Juice

½ oz. blueberry schnapps
½ oz. Chambord
½ oz. vodka
Splash blue curaçao
Splash cranberry juice

 JUDI NORTH • MARGATE, NJ

Grape Juicer

1 part 99 Grapes
1 part triple sec

Grape Lax

1 oz. Chambord
1 oz. blue curaçao
Splash 7-Up
Splash cranberry juice

Build.

Grape Nehi

1 ¾ oz. Absolut Kurant vodka
¾ oz. cranberry juice
Splash club soda

Shake with ice, and strain into a shot glass. Top
with club soda.

Grasshopper

2 parts half-and-half or milk
1 part green crème de menthe
1 part vodka
1 part white crème de cacao

Shake with ice, and strain into a shot glass.

Great Balls of Fire

½ oz. Goldschläger
½ oz. cinnamon schnapps
½ oz. cherry brandy

Layer in a shot glass.

Greek Fire

1 oz. brandy
½ oz. Metaxa ouzo

Build.

Greek Revolution

½ oz. grenadine
½ oz. Metaxa ouzo
½ oz. Galliano

Pour grenadine into a shooter glass. Carefully float ouzo, then Galliano to form three layers. Do not stir.

Green Apple

½ oz. apple schnapps
½ oz. Midori melon liqueur
¼ oz. sweet and sour mix
Dash 7-Up

Shake the first three ingredients with ice and strain into a shot glass. Top with 7-Up.

Green Bullet

¾ oz. green crème de menthe
¾ oz. white crème de menthe
½ oz. Bacardi 151 rum

Shake with ice, and strain into a shot glass.

Green Demon

½ oz. Bacardi rum
½ oz. lemonade
½ oz. Midori melon liqueur
½ oz. Smirnoff vodka

Shake with ice, and strain into a shot glass.

Green Devil

1 ½ oz. Beefeater gin
¼ oz. Hiram Walker green crème de menthe
Splash Rose's lime juice

Shake with ice, and strain into a shot glass.

Green Dragon

1 oz. green Chartreuse
½ oz. Bacardi 151 rum

Build.

Green Genie

1 oz. green Chartreuse
1 oz. tequila
Splash Tabasco

Shake with ice, and strain into a shot glass.

Green Hornet

¾ oz. green crème de menthe
¾ oz. Southern Comfort

Shake with ice, and strain into a shot glass.

Green Lantern

½ oz. Cointreau
¾ oz. green Chartreuse liqueur
¾ oz. vodka

Shake with ice, and strain into a shot glass.

Green Lizard

1 part Bacardi 151 rum
1 part green Chartreuse
Splash lime juice

Shake with ice, and strain into a shot glass.

Green Meanie

¾ oz. Midori melon liqueur
¾ oz. Southern Comfort
Splash pineapple juice

Shake with ice, and strain into a shot glass.

Green Slime

1 part Bacardi rum
1 part Midori melon liqueur
1 part orange juice
1 part pineapple juice
1 part Smirnoff vodka

Blend and strain into a shot glass. "If you can't do the time, don't drink the slime."

 TINY, DR. OF MIXOLOGY • MCB'S PUB • SKOKIE, IL

Green Snake

1 oz. DeKuyper Sour Apple Pucker
    schnapps
½ oz. Sprite
½ oz. Three Olives cherry vodka

Shake with ice, and strain into a chilled shot glass.

 JONATHAN LAWRENCE • CHESAPEAKE, VA

Green Sneaker

2 oz. orange juice
1 oz. Frïs vodka
½ oz. Hiram Walker triple sec
½ oz. Midori melon liqueur

Shake with ice, and strain into a shot glass.

Green Spider

1 oz. dark crème de menthe
1 oz. white crème de cacao

Shake with ice, and strain into a shot glass.

Green Weenie

1 part Jose Cuervo Gold tequila
1 part Midori melon liqueur
1 part sweet and sour mix

Build.

 PAT ENSTEN • BRANNIGANS SPORTS BAR AND
GRILL • STILLWATER, OK

Greg's Warm Apple Pie Shooter

½ oz. Berentzen liqueur
½ oz. DeKuyper Sour Apple Pucker
  schnapps
¼ oz. butterscotch schnapps

 GREG MUSANTRY • BARNEGAT, NJ

Gremlin

1 oz. Absolut vodka
¼ oz. Bacardi rum
¼ oz. blue curaçao
¼ oz. orange juice

Shake with ice, and strain into a shot glass.

G-Spot

½ oz. amaretto
½ oz. Midori melon liqueur
¼ oz. Cointreau
Splash pineapple juice
Splash sweet and sour mix

 COREY MELENDREZ • LAS VEGAS, NV

Guillotine

¾ oz. Smirnoff vodka
½ oz. Rumble Minze peppermint schnapps
½ oz. Sauza tequila

Shake with ice, and strain into a shot glass.

Gum Drop

3 oz. pineapple juice
1 ½ oz. Galliano
1 oz. Disaronno amaretto
1 oz. Licor 43
Splash grenadine

Shake with ice, and strain into a shot glass.
Serves two.

 STEVEN COTSORADIS, JR. • GARDEN BAR •
BALTIMORE, MD

Gumby

1 ¼ oz. Frïs vodka
½ oz. Midori melon liqueur
¼ oz. 7-Up

Shake the first two ingredients with ice and strain into a shot glass. Top with 7-Up.

Hairy Navel

1 part Absolut vodka
1 part DeKuyper Peachtree schnapps
2 parts orange juice

Build.

Half and Half

1 part Fürst Bismarck
1 part Schöenauer Apfel schnapps, chilled

Pour the ingredients into a shot glass.

Halloween Shooter

¾ oz. Licor 43
¾ oz. Opal Nera black sambuca

Build.

Happy Camper

1 part Absolut Citron vodka
1 part DeKuyper Peachtree schnapps
1 part DeKuyper Sour Apple Pucker
    schnapps
Splash 7-Up
Splash orange juice

 CAROLYN LEMICE • LAS VEGAS, NV

Happy Jack

1 ½ oz. Jack Daniel's whiskey
½ oz. apple schnapps

Shake with ice, and strain into a shot glass.

Harbor Lights

1 part Galliano
1 part Rémy Martin cognac

Build.

Harbor Lights #2

¾ oz. Galliano
¼ oz. Metaxa 5-Star Brandy

Build.

Harbor Lights #3

¾ oz. Chambord
¾ oz. rum
½ oz. orange juice

Shake with ice, and strain into a shot glass.

Harbor Lights #4

½ oz. amaretto
½ oz. Caffé Lolita liqueur
½ oz. Southern Comfort
½ oz. Bacardi 151 rum

Build.

Harbor Lights #5

½ oz. green crème de menthe
½ oz. Jack Daniel's Black Label whiskey
½ oz. grenadine

Build.

Harbor Mist

½ oz. Myers's Original dark rum
½ oz. orange juice
½ oz. pineapple juice
½ oz. Tia Maria

Shake with ice, and strain into a shot glass.

Harvey's Hot Shot

¾ oz. Galliano
¾ oz. orange juice
Whipped cream to top

Pour Galliano and orange juice into a shaker.
Pour unstrained into a shot glass and top with
whipped cream.

Hawaiian Punch

½ oz. amaretto
½ oz. orange juice
½ oz. pineapple juice
½ oz. Southern Comfort
Dash grenadine

Add grenadine to color. Shake with ice, and
strain into a shot glass.

Hawaiian Punch #2

½ oz. crème de almond
½ oz. Southern Comfort
¼ oz. pineapple juice
¼ oz. Smirnoff 100 vodka

Shake with ice, and strain into a shot glass.

Hawaiian Punch #3

¾ oz. Southern Comfort
½ oz. orange juice
¼ oz. Cointreau
¼ oz. Hiram Walker sloe gin

Shake with ice, and strain into a shot glass.

Hay Shothead

1 ½ oz. Three Olives pomegranate vodka
¼ oz. Tabasco

Shoot.

 YELOF YAR • EDGAR, NJ

Head

¾ oz. Hiram Walker root beer schnapps
¾ oz. half-and-half

Layer.

Head Room

¼ oz. Hiram Walker crème de banana
¼ oz. Midori melon liqueur
½ oz. Carolans Irish cream

Build.

Head Rush

¼ oz. Chambord
¼ oz. pear schnapps
¼ oz. peach schnapps
¼ oz. Romana sambuca
¼ oz. Galliano
¼ oz. Baileys Irish cream

Serve in a shot glass. Build. Float Baileys last.

 DAVID WILLETT • DAYS INN • FIRESIDE LOUNGE •
SO. PORTLAND, ME

Heather's Hot Flash

½ oz. Absolut vodka
½ oz. Kahlúa
½ oz. DeKuyper Buttershot schnapps
Baileys Irish cream to float

Build the first three ingredients. Float Baileys on top.

 HEATHER HOWIE • EASTON, PA

Heavy Metal

1 part Goldschläger, chilled
1 part Jägermeister, chilled

Build.

 DAN CULLIGAN • FORT COLLINS COUNTRY CLUB
• FORT COLLINS, CO

Hide the Banana

½ oz. Frïs vodka
½ oz. Hiram Walker amaretto
½ oz. Midori melon liqueur

Shake with ice, and strain into a shot glass.

High Jamaican Wind

1 oz. Myers's Original dark rum
⅓ oz. Kahlúa
Half-and-half to float

Build the first two ingredients; float half-and-half on top.

Hit and Run

1 oz. Bombay gin
1 oz. anisette

Build.

Hollywood

¾ oz. Chambord
¾ oz. Finlandia vodka
½ oz. pineapple juice

Shake with ice, and strain into a shot glass.

Hometown Comfort

½ oz. Frangelico
½ oz. Southern Comfort
½ oz. Kahlúa

Shake the first two ingredients with ice and strain into a shot glass. Pour in Kahlúa. It will sink to the bottom.

 MOISES & JASON • BUC O'BRIANS • FREDERICKSBURG, TX

Honeysuckle Shooter

1 oz. Bacardi rum
Splash simple syrup
Splash sweet and sour mix

Shake with ice, and strain into a shot glass.

Hooter

½ oz. Frïs vodka
½ oz. grenadine
½ oz. Hiram Walker amaretto
½ oz. orange juice

Shake with ice, and strain into a shot glass.

Horny Lil' Indian

¾ oz. Absolut vodka
¼ oz. Cointreau
¼ oz. grenadine
¼ oz. orange juice
Splash tequila

Shake with ice, and strain into a shot glass.

 RORY L. CHATMAN • NORFOLK, VA

Horny Monkey

¼ oz. Baileys Irish cream
¼ oz. crème de banana
¼ oz. green crème de menthe
¼ oz. Kahlúa

Horny Wally

1 ½ oz. curaçao
½ oz. Bacardi rum
½ oz. Midori melon liqueur
Splash 7-Up
Splash sweet and sour mix

 GREG COHEN • ROCKVILLE, MD

Hot Beach Shooter

¾ oz. Malibu rum
¾ oz. peach schnapps
1 oz. coffee

Build.

Hot Cherry Pie

1 oz. amaretto
½ oz. cranberry juice

Shake with ice, and strain into a shot glass.

Hot Goose

1 ½ oz. Grand Marnier
½ oz. hot water

Shake and strain into a shot glass.

Hot Houdini

3 drops Tabasco
2 oz. Fernet Branca

Serve in a shot glass. Make it disappear fast.

 THE MURPH • SPRING LAKE HEIGHTS, NJ

Hot Lava

1 ¼ oz. Absolut Peppar vodka
¼ oz. Disaronno amaretto

Build.

Hot Monkey Love

⅓ oz. Baileys Irish cream
⅓ oz. crème de banana
⅓ oz. Original Bartenders Cocktails Hot Sex

 ADAM POWELL • MADISON, WI

Hot Nuts

1 ½ oz. Frangelico
½ oz. hot water
Whipped cream to top

Build the first two ingredients. Top with whipped cream.

Hot Shot

¾ oz. Jameson Irish whiskey
¾ oz. Baileys Irish cream
½ oz. hot coffee

Build.

Hot Shot #2

¾ oz. Baileys Irish cream
¾ oz. Grand Marnier
½ oz. coffee

Hot Shot #3

½ oz. Stolichnaya vodka
½ oz. Rumple Minze peppermint schnapps
Few drops Tabasco

Build.

Hot Shot #4

1 oz. Hiram Walker sambuca
½ oz. Carolans Irish cream
Splash coffee

Build.

Hot Stuff

1 oz. coffee
1 oz. Hiram Walker amaretto

Serve in 2-oz. shot glass.

Hot "T"

2 oz. Tarantula Reposado tequila
3 dashes Tabasco

Serve as a shot.

Hot Tamale

¾ oz. cinnamon schnapps
½ oz. Jose Cuervo Gold tequila

Build.

Hot Tamale #2

1 ½ oz. Goldschläger
⅛ oz. Grenadine
2 Red Hots candies for garnish

Blend the first two ingredients with ice and serve
in a shot glass. Garnish with Red Hots.

I Love Lucy

¾ oz. Malibu rum
¾ oz. sloe gin
Splash orange juice
Splash Sprite

 PAM PAYTON • ST. ROBERTS, MO

Ice Blue Aqua Velva

¾ oz. Bombay gin
¾ oz. Stolichnaya vodka
½ oz. blue curaçao
Splash 7-Up

Shake the first three ingredients with ice. Top with 7-Up.

Ice Caps

¾ oz. Absolut vodka
¾ oz. Rumple Minze peppermint schnapps

Shake with ice, and strain into a shot glass.

Ice Pick

1 part Stolichnaya vodka
3 parts iced tea
Splash sweet and sour mix

Build.

Iceberg Shooter

1 ½ oz. Frïs vodka
½ oz. Hiram Walker peppermint schnapps

Shake with ice, and strain into a shot glass.

Icebreaker

1 oz. Rumple Minze peppermint schnapps
1 oz. Yukon Jack whiskey

Build.

Iced Blues

1 oz. blueberry schnapps
½ oz. blue curaçao

Shake with ice, and strain into a shot glass.

 ALICE SHANK • NATALIE'S • SYRACUSE, NY

Illusion Shooter

1 part Absolut vodka
1 part peach schnapps
Splash cranberry juice
Splash orange juice

Shake with ice, and strain into a shot glass.

Indian Summer

½ oz. Kahlúa
½ oz. pineapple juice
½ oz. Stolichnaya vodka

Shake with ice, and strain into a shot glass.

Indigo

1 oz. Stolichnaya Razberi vodka
½ oz. DeKuyper Peachtree schnapps
¼ oz. blue curaçao
¼ oz. Chambord
Splash 7-Up

Shake with ice, and strain into a chilled shot glass.

 RYAN WILLIAMS • THE COPPER • DOUGLAS, MI

Ink Spot

¾ oz. blackberry brandy
¼ oz. Rumple Minze peppermint schnapps

Shake with ice, and strain into a shot glass.

Inoculation Shot

1 oz. Jose Cuervo Gold tequila
¼ oz. DeKuyper blue curaçao

Shake with ice, and strain into a shot glass.

International

¾ oz. Galliano
½ oz. Asbach Uralt brandy

Shake with ice, and strain into a shot glass.

International Incident

¼ oz. Absolut vodka
¼ oz. Baileys Irish cream
¼ oz. Disaronno amaretto
¼ oz. Frangelico
¼ oz. Kahlúa

Shake with ice, and strain into a shot glass.

Irish Brogue

1 oz. Jameson Irish whiskey
¼ oz. Irish Mist liqueur

Build.

Irish Charlie

1 oz. Baileys Irish cream
1 oz. white crème de menthe

Stir with ice, and strain into a cordial glass.

Irish Flag

1 oz. green crème de menthe
1 oz. Baileys Irish cream
1 oz. Grand Marnier

Layer in order in a cordial glass.

Irish Frog

¾ oz. Midori melon liqueur
¾ oz. Baileys Irish cream, chilled

Build.

Irish Frost

1 ½ oz. Baileys Irish cream
Splash Coco López cream of coconut
Splash half-and-half

Shake with ice, and strain into a shot glass.

Irish Headlock

1 oz. Baileys Irish cream
¼ oz. Jameson Irish whiskey
¼ oz. Disaronno amaretto
¼ oz. brandy

Build.

Irish Kiss

1 oz. Baileys Irish cream
½ oz. Jameson Irish whiskey
½ oz. Irish Mist liqueur

Shake with ice, and strain into a shot glass.

Irish Melon Ball

¾ oz. Baileys Irish cream
½ oz. Midori melon liqueur
½ oz. vodka

Build.

Irish Quaalude

½ oz. Carolans Irish cream
½ oz. Frangelico
½ oz. Frïs vodka
½ oz. Hiram Walker white crème de cacao

Shake with ice, and strain into a shot glass.

Irish Raspberry

1 part Chambord
1 part Devonshire Royal cream liqueur

Shake with ice, and strain into a shot glass.

Irish Rule

1 part Carolans Irish cream
1 part Irish Mist liqueur

Build.

Irish Setter

½ oz. Irish Mist liqueur
½ oz. Frangelico
¼ oz. Rumple Minze peppermint schnapps
¼ oz. brandy

Build.

Irish Sleeper

1 oz. Jameson Irish whiskey
½ oz. Grand Marnier
½ oz. Irish Mist liqueur

Shake with ice, and strain into a shot glass.

Irish Trinity

1 oz. Tullamore Dew Irish whiskey
½ oz. Carolans Irish cream
½ oz. Irish Mist

Serve as a shot.

 RON CARROLL • ALICE'S • EASTON, PA

Iron Butterfly

½ oz. Carolans Irish cream
½ oz. Frïs vodka
½ oz. Kahlúa

Shake with ice, and strain into a shot glass. Serve straight up.

Iron Cross

¾ oz. apricot brandy
¾ oz. Rumple Minze peppermint schnapps

Shake with ice, and strain into a shot glass.

It Don't Matter

1 ¾ oz. Wild Turkey bourbon
Grand Marnier to float

Italian Flag Shooter

1 part crème de strawberry
1 part green crème de menthe
1 part Baileys Irish cream

Layer in order.

Italian Root Beer (Root Beer Shooter)

1 part cola
1 part Galliano

Italian Russian

½ oz. Romana sambuca
1 oz. Stolichnaya vodka

Build.

Italian Spear

1 part Hiram Walker peppermint schnapps
1 part Hiram Walker amaretto

Build.

Jack Frost

1 oz. Jack Daniel's whiskey
1 oz. peppermint schnapps

Jack Hammer

½ oz. Jack Daniel's Old No. 7 whiskey
½ oz. DeKuyper Hot Damn! cinnamon
  schnapps
½ oz. Midori melon liqueur

Layer in shot glass.

 MATT MEYERS • MARY'S BISTRO • MACKINAC
ISLAND, MI

Jack O'Lantern

½ oz. amaretto
½ oz. orange juice
½ oz. pineapple juice
½ oz. Southern Comfort
Dash grenadine

Shake with ice, and strain into a shot glass.

Jack Rabbit

¾ oz. Yukon Jack whiskey
½ oz. cherry brandy

Shake with ice, and strain into a shot glass.

Jägasm

1 part Absolut vodka
1 part amaretto
1 part Jägermeister
1 part Kahlúa
Splash Baileys Irish cream
Splash grenadine
Heavy cream to top

Shake the first six ingredients. Top with heavy cream.

Jäger Barrel

1 part Jägermeister
1 part root beer schnapps
1 part cola

Build.

Jäger Eraser

1 part Jägermeister
1 part Absolut vodka
1 part club soda

Build.

Jäger Monster

2 parts orange juice
1 part Jägermeister
Dash grenadine

Shake with crushed ice until smooth and strain
into a shot glass.

Jäger Ron

½ oz. Baileys Irish cream
½ oz. crème de cacao
½ oz. crème de menthe
½ oz. Jägermeister

Shake with ice, and strain into a shot glass.

 RON VILLA • THE BREAK ROOM LOUNGE •
MAUMEE, OH

Jäger Vacation

2 parts pineapple juice
1 part Captain Morgan coconut rum
1 part Jägermeister

Shake with ice, and strain into a shot glass.

Jägerita

½ oz. Cointreau
½ oz. Jägermeister
½ oz. tequila
Juice of ½ lime
Salt to rim glass

Shake. Strain into a shot glass with a salted rim.

Jäger-ita

¾ oz. Cointreau
¼ oz. Jägermeister
¼ oz. Rose's lime juice
¼ oz. sweet and sour mix

 KIM ANDERSEN • NEW YORK, NY

Jagertee Hot Shot

1 part hot water
1 part Stroh Jagertee

Serve in a shot glass.

Jamaican 10 Speed

½ oz. crème de banana
½ oz. Malibu rum
½ oz. Midori melon liqueur
½ oz. milk or half-and-half
½ oz. pineapple juice

 KEYHOLE BAR & GRILL • MACKINAW CITY, MI

Jamaican Dust

¾ oz. Puerto Rican rum
¾ oz. Tia Maria
Splash pineapple juice

Build.

Jamaican Lollipop Shooter

1 ½ oz. crème de banana
½ oz. Bacardi 151 rum

Shake with ice, and strain into a shot glass.

Jamaican Sunrise

¾ oz. Cointreau
¾ oz. Myers's rum cream
½ oz. sweet and sour mix

Shake with ice, and strain into a shot glass.

Jamaican Surfer

2 parts half-and-half
2 parts Malibu rum
1 part Tia Maria

Shake with ice, and strain into a shot glass.

Jambalaya

½ oz. peach schnapps
½ oz. Southern Comfort
½ oz. sweet and sour mix
Drop grenadine

 GINA & JANET • THE APPROACH •
SADDLEBACK LANES • MISSION VIEJO, CA

Jaw Breaker

1 ½ oz. Goldschläger
Dash Tabasco

Shake with ice, and strain into a shot glass.

Je T'aime

¾ oz. B&B liqueur
¾ oz. Absolut vodka

Build.

Jefferson Blues

1 part Absolut vodka
1 part blue curaçao
1 part DeKuyper WilderBerry schnapps
1 part Rose's sweet and sour mix
Splash Sprite or 7-Up

Shake with ice, and strain into a shot glass.

 LORI JOHNSON • JEFFERSON GRILLE •
WARWICK, RI

Jekyll & Hyde

1 oz. Jägermeister, cold
1 oz. Dr. McGillicuddy's Mentholmint
    schnapps, cold

Layer in test-tube shot glass.

 JOE WILLETT • SCOTTSDALE, AZ

Jell-O Shots

1 cup boiling water
1 cup liquor of your choice, such as tequila,
    vodka, gin, or rum
1 3-oz. box lime Jell-O brand gelatin
3–4 oz. lime juice

In a bowl, add the gelatin to the liquor and boiling water. Stir until the gelatin has dissolved. Chill to set. Serve in paper soufflé cups.

Jelly Bean

Splash grenadine
½ oz. sambuca
½ oz. Jose Cuervo Especial tequila

Layer.

Jelly Bean #2

⅓ oz. grenadine
⅓ oz. anisette
⅓ oz. tequila

Build.

Jelly Bean #3

¾ oz. blackberry brandy
¾ oz. amaretto
¼ oz. Southern Comfort

Build.

Jelly Bean #4

1 oz. blackberry brandy
¾ oz. Romana sambuca

Build.

Jelly Bean #5

¾ oz. Southern Comfort
½ oz. anisette
½ oz. grenadine

Build.

Jelly Donut

1 oz. Chambord
½ oz. half-and-half

Shake with ice, and strain into a shot glass.

Jelly Fish

¾ oz. Romana sambuca
¾ oz. Baileys Irish cream
3 drops grenadine

Build.

Jelly Fish #2

1 part white crème de cacao
1 part Baileys Irish cream
1 part Disaronno amaretto
Dash grenadine

Build, with the dash of grenadine in the center.

Jethro Tull Flute

1 oz. DeKuyper Peachtree schnapps
1 oz. Finlandia vodka
½ oz. Cointreau
Splash pineapple juice

 BONNIE S. BAILEY • WAPPINGERS FALLS, NY

Jimmy's Juice

½ oz. Captain Morgan rum
½ oz. cranberry juice
½ oz. Malibu rum
½ oz. pineapple juice

Shake with ice, and strain into a shot glass.

Johnny on the Beach

1 ½ oz. Finlandia vodka
1 oz. Chambord
1 oz. Midori melon liqueur
½ oz. cranberry juice
½ oz. grapefruit juice
½ oz. orange juice
½ oz. pineapple juice

Shake with ice, and strain into a shot glass.
Serves two.

Jolly Rancher

1 oz. peach schnapps
½ oz. apple schnapps
½ oz. cranberry juice

Shake with ice, and strain into a shot glass.

Jolly Rancher #2

1 oz. cranberry juice
½ oz. Midori melon liqueur
½ oz. peach schnapps

Shake with ice, and strain into a shot glass.

Juicy Fruit

1 oz. vodka
½ oz. pineapple juice
¼ oz. Midori melon liqueur
¼ oz. peach schnapps

Shake with ice, and strain into a shot glass.

Junior Mint

¾ oz. Godiva chocolate liqueur
¾ oz. Rumple Minze peppermint schnapps

 JOHN KYLE • PITTSBURGH, PA

Kahlúa Surfer

2 parts Malibu rum
1 part half-and-half
1 part Kahlúa

Shake with ice, and strain into a shot glass.

Kaisermeister

1 part Jägermeister
1 part root beer schnapps

Shake with ice, and strain into a shot glass.

Kamikazi

1 ½ oz. Stolichnaya vodka
¼ oz. Cointreau
Splash Rose's lime juice

Shake with ice, and strain into a shot glass.

Kandy Kane

1 part Rumple Minze peppermint schnapps
1 part Hiram Walker crème de noyaux

Build.

Kaytusha Rocker

1 oz. Frïs vodka
1 oz. pineapple juice
½ oz. Kahlúa
Dash half-and-half

Shake with ice, and strain into a shot glass.

Ke Largo

¾ oz. KeKe Beach
¾ oz. Midori melon liqueur

Shake with ice, and strain into a shot glass.

Keelhaul

1 shot Sailor Jerry Spiced Navy rum
Lime wedge
Sugar

Coat the lime wedge with sugar. Shoot the rum
and chase with the lime.

Keno Koolaid

½ oz. Southern Comfort
½ oz. vodka
¼ oz. Chambord
¼ oz. Cointreau
¼ oz. grenadine

 LISA NADOLNY & KEN SANTOS • NARRAGANSETT, RI

Kentucky Colonel

1 oz. Wild Turkey bourbon
¼ oz. Benedictine

Shake with ice, and strain into a shot glass.

Key Lime High

½ oz. Cointreau
½ oz. Galliano
½ oz. orange juice
Splash half-and-half
Splash lime juice

Shake with ice, and strain into a shot glass.
Serves two.

Key Lime Pie

1 ½ oz. Licor 43
½ oz. half-and-half
Dash Rose's lime juice
Dash sweet and sour mix

Shake with ice, and strain into a shot glass.

Kicken Chicken

¾ oz. Rumple Minze peppermint schnapps
¾ oz. Wild Turkey bourbon

Shake with ice, and strain into a shot glass.

KilleCream

1 oz. Carolans Irish cream
1 oz. Killepitsch herbal liqueur

Shake with ice, and serve in a shot glass.

Killepitsch Ice-Cold

1 shot Killepitsch herbal liqueur

Serve straight up and chilled with your favorite
beer on the side.

 P. NELSON • MADISON, NJ

Killer Bee

¾ oz. Jägermeister
¾ oz. Schönauer Apfel schnapps

Shake with ice, and strain into a shot glass.

Killer Kool-Aid

1 oz. Absolut vodka
½ oz. cranberry juice
¼ oz. Disaronno amaretto
¼ oz. Midori melon liqueur

Shake with ice, and strain into a shot glass.

Killer Oreos

1 part Baileys Irish cream
1 part Jägermeister
1 part Kahlúa

Shake with ice, and strain into a shot glass.

Kilt Lifter

1 part Baileys Irish cream
1 part butterscotch schnapps

Build.

Kilted Black Leprechaun

2 parts Irish cream
1 part Bacardi 8 rum
1 part Drambuie

Shake with ice, and strain into a shot glass. Serve in a shot glass.

King Alphonse

1 ½ oz. dark crème de cacao
½ oz. half-and-half

Build.

Kiss in the Dark

¾ oz. cherry brandy
¾ oz. Tanqueray gin
¼ oz. dry vermouth

Shake with ice, and strain into a shot glass.

Kiwi Kicker

½ oz. Disaronno amaretto
½ oz. Midori melon liqueur
½ oz. Yukon Jack whiskey
¾ oz. cranberry juice
¾ oz. pineapple juice

Shake the first three ingredients with ice and strain into a shot glass. Fill with juice.

 SCOTT KARG • LOUGHLIN'S CHESAPEAKE PUB • EDGEWOOD, MD

Knickerbocker

½ oz. Frïs vodka
½ oz. Hiram Walker amaretto
½ oz. Hiram Walker peppermint schnapps
½ oz. Kahlúa

Shake with ice, and strain into a shot glass.

K.O. Pectate

⅓ oz. half-and-half
⅓ oz. Kahlúa
⅓ oz. peppermint schnapps

Kool-Aid

¾ oz. amaretto
¾ oz. Midori melon liqueur
½ oz. cranberry juice

Shake with ice, and strain into a shot glass.

Krazy Kool-Aid

1 part Disaronno amaretto
1 part Finlandia cranberry vodka
1 part Midori melon liqueur

Shake with ice, and strain into a shot glass.

Kurant Affair

1 oz. Absolut Kurant vodka
½ oz. pineapple juice
Scant splash cranberry juice

Kurant Kooler

1 ¼ oz. Absolut Kurant vodka
½ oz. sweet and sour mix
Splash 7-Up

Shake vodka and sweet and sour mix. Top with
7-Up.

Kurant Shooter

1 oz. pineapple juice
½ oz. Absolut Kurant vodka
½ oz. Midori melon liqueur

Shake with ice, and strain into a shot glass.

La Cucaracha

½ oz. Kahlúa
½ oz. Jose Cuervo tequila
½ oz. bottled mineral water

Build.

Lady Godiva

¾ oz. Grand Marnier
¾ oz. Kahlúa
½ oz. half-and-half

Shake with ice, and strain into a shot glass.

Lake Martin Slammer

2 oz. Crown Royal whiskey
¼ oz. grenadine
Splash cranberry juice

Shake, strain, and shoot.

 PHILIP DEAN, RODNEY DEAN, & SHEP SAVAGE •
SINCLAIRE'S (KAWLIGA) AND PAUL LAKEY •
DOCKSIDE GRILLE, LAKE MARTIN, AL

Lala's Lumps

1 part Finlandia vodka
1 part root beer schnapps

Build.

Landshark

1 ¼ oz. Stubbs Australian rum
¾ oz. Malibu rum
¼ oz. pineapple juice
Splash grenadine

Shake with ice, and strain into a shot glass.

Landslide

⅓ part Baileys Irish cream
⅓ part crème de banana
⅓ part Disaronno amaretto

Shake with ice, and strain into a shot glass.

Laser Beam

½ oz. Jack Daniel's whiskey
½ oz. Rumple Minze peppermint schnapps
¼ oz. Drambuie

Shake with ice, and strain into a shot glass.

Laser Beam #2

¾ oz. Jack Daniel's whiskey
½ oz. anisette
Dash grenadine

Shake with ice, and strain into a shot glass.

Laser Disc

½ oz. Dewar's White Label blended scotch
   whisky
½ oz. Drambuie
½ oz. lemonade

Shake. Serve in a shot glass.

Lava Lamp

2 parts Rumple Minze peppermint
   schnapps, chilled
1 part Absolut Peppar vodka
7 drops Tabasco
Draft beer, cold

Use very cold Rumple Minze. Drop in Tabasco
carefully to form floating balls in the middle of
the liqueur. Serve with a cold draft beer back.

 JESSICA LEE • INTERNATIONAL COCKTAIL LOUNGE
• SAN FRANCISCO, CA

Leg Spreader Shooter

1 part Galliano
1 part Kahlúa

Shake with ice, and strain into a shot glass.

Lemon Drop

1 ¼ oz. Absolut Citron vodka
Lemon wedge
Sugar to coat lemon wedge

Serve with a wedge of lemon coated with sugar.
Shoot Absolut Citron, then suck the lemon.

Lemon Drop #2

1 oz. Stolichnaya vodka
Dash Cointreau
Lemon wheel
Powdered sugar for garnish

Place the lemon wheel over a shot glass. Top with powdered sugar.

Lemonade Cactus

1 oz. DeKuyper cactus juice liqueur
1 oz. lemonade

Shake with ice, and strain into a shot glass.

Leprechaun Shooter

¾ oz. blue curaçao
¾ oz. orange juice
¾ oz. peach schnapps

Shake with ice, and strain into a shot glass.

Lethal Weapon

1 oz. Finlandia vodka
½ oz. peach schnapps
Splash cranberry juice
Splash Rose's lime juice

Shake with ice, and strain into a shot glass.

Library Ladder

½ oz. Baileys Irish cream
½ oz. Grand Marnier
½ oz. Licor 43

Shake and serve straight up as a shot.

 RYAN MAYBEE • PIERPONT'S AT UNION STATION •
KANSAS CITY, MO

Licorice Lix

¾ oz. sambuca
¼ oz. orange juice

Licorice Stick

¾ oz. Licor 43
½ oz. Cointreau
½ oz. half-and-half
Dash sweet and sour mix

Shake with ice, and strain into a shot glass.

Licorice Stick #2

1 ¼ oz. Stolichnaya vodka
½ oz. Hiram Walker anisette
¼ oz. Cointreau

Shake with ice, and strain into a shot glass.

Life Saver

1 part Malibu rum
1 part Smirnoff vodka
1 part Midori melon liqueur
1 part 7-Up or Sprite (optional)

Build.

Lighthouse

1 part Kahlúa
1 part Bacardi 151 rum

Build.

Limo Rider

1 oz. Fernet Branca
½ oz. Borghetti sambuca
½ oz. Seagram's vodka

Serve as a shot.

Lion Tamer

¾ oz. Southern Comfort
¼ oz. Rose's lime juice

Fill a mixing glass with ice. Add ingredients and stir. Strain into a chilled shot glass.

Liquid Babysitter

½ oz. Absolut vodka
½ oz. Captain Morgan rum
Splash 7-Up
Splash DeKuyper Apple Pucker schnapps
Splash DeKuyper Cherry Pucker schnapps
Splash DeKuyper Grape Pucker schnapps
Splash DeKuyper Watermelon Pucker schnapps

 CHRISTIN "CK" KOTILA • WARREN, MI

Liquid Cocaine

½ oz. Disaronno amaretto
½ oz. Grand Marnier
½ oz. Southern Comfort
Splash orange juice
Splash pineapple juice

Shake with ice, and strain into a shot glass.

Liquid Nitrogen

1 part Ouzo 12
1 part Romana sambuca

Mix and strain over ice.

Liquid Quaalude

1 ½ oz. Stolichnaya vodka
¼ oz. Southern Comfort
⅛ oz. crème de noyaux
½ splash orange juice
½ splash pineapple juice

Shake with ice, and strain into a shot glass.

Liquid Valium

1 ¼ oz. Frïs vodka
½ oz. Hiram Walker peppermint schnapps

Shake with ice, and strain into a shot glass.

Little Beer

¾ oz. Licor 43
¼ oz. half-and-half

Float half-and-half on top.

Little Purple Man

1 oz. sambuca
1 oz. Chambord raspberry liqueur

Build.

Loch Ness Monster

¾ oz. Midori melon liqueur
¾ oz. Baileys Irish cream
¼ oz. Jägermeister

Build.

Loco Lobo

1 part Galliano
1 part Jose Cuervo tequila
1 part lime juice

Locomotive Breath

1 oz. J&B scotch whisky
1 oz. Jose Cuervo tequila
½ oz. Bacardi dark rum
Splash ginger ale

Stir, don't shake. Pour into a highball glass, no ice.

 BONNIE S. BAILEY • WAPPINGERS FALLS, NY

Long Island Shooter

1 part Absolut vodka
1 part Bacardi rum
1 part Beefeater gin
1 part Cointreau
1 part Jose Cuervo tequila
1 part sweet and sour mix
Splash Coke

Shake the first six ingredients with ice and strain into a shot glass. Top with Coke.

Loose Moose

½ oz. Galliano
½ oz. peach schnapps
¼ oz. Cointreau
Splash lemonade

Chill in a 2-oz. shot glass.

Lounge Lizard

2 parts Myers's Original dark rum
1 part orange juice
1 part pineapple juice
1 part sweet and sour mix
Splash grenadine

Shake with ice, and strain into a shot glass.

Love Potion #9

1 oz. cranberry juice
¾ oz. cherry brandy
¾ oz. Rumple Minze peppermint schnapps

Shake with ice, and strain into a shot glass.

Love Shack

1 ¼ oz. Myers's Original dark rum
¼ oz. orange juice
¼ oz. grenadine
7-Up to top

Build first three ingredients. Top with 7-Up.

Low Rider

1 ½ oz. Tarantula Reposado tequila
½ oz. McCormick triple sec
Splash cranberry juice

Shake and serve in a shot glass.

Lucky Seven

1 part amaretto
1 part Bacardi 151 rum
1 part Jack Daniel's whiskey
1 part sloe gin
1 part Southern Comfort
1 part vodka
Splash cranberry juice
Splash lime juice
Splash orange juice

Serve in a very big shot glass.

 JOEL GAGNE • LOWELL, MA

Lust in the Dust

¾ oz. Original Bartenders Cocktails Hot Sex
¼ oz. Kahlúa

 SUSIE VILES • DENISON, TX

Lymbo

½ oz. Bacardi dark rum
½ oz. Hiram Walker cinnamon schnapps
½ oz. tequila
Splash Tabasco

Shake with ice, and strain into a shot glass.

 NOREEN MAES • LUCKIE'S • SPARKS, NV

Lynchburg Lemonade Shooter

¾ oz. Jack Daniel's whiskey
½ oz. sweet and sour mix
¼ oz. Cointreau

Shake with ice, and strain into a shot glass.

M&M

1 oz. Kahlúa
1 oz. Disaronno amaretto

Build.

Mad Cow

¾ oz. Opal Nera black sambuca
¼ oz. Godiva chocolate liqueur
Splash milk

 DAVID `BUCKWHEAT` CAVALIERE •
N. PROVIDENCE, RI

Madras Shooter

1 oz. Absolut vodka
½ oz. orange juice
½ oz. cranberry juice

Build. Substitute grapefruit juice for orange juice
and it's a Sea Breeze Shooter.

Malibu Classic

1 oz. Stolichnaya vodka
½ oz. Malibu rum
¼ oz. cranberry juice
¼ oz. orange juice

Shake with ice, and strain into a shot glass.

Malibu Sex on the Beach

½ oz. cranberry juice
½ oz. Frïs vodka
½ oz. Hiram Walker peach schnapps

Stir with ice, and strain into a shot glass.

Manhattan Project

¼ oz. amaretto
¼ oz. peppermint schnapps
¼ oz. Southern Comfort
¼ oz. white tequila

 NICK VANDENBROUCKE • SAN DIEGO, CA

Marie Brizard Ecstasy

1 part Marie Brizard cherry liqueur
1 part Marie Brizard peach liqueur
1 part Marie Brizard pear liqueur
Orange juice to fill
Splash cranberry juice

Build the first three ingredients. Fill to the top with orange juice; add a splash of cranberry juice.

Marie Brizard Sun 'N Fun

1 part Marie Brizard Cointreau
1 part Marie Brizard coconut liqueur
1 part Marie Brizard mango liqueur
Pineapple juice to fill
Drop grenadine

Build the first three ingredients. Fill the balance of the shooter tube or glass with pineapple juice. Pour a drop of grenadine on top. Shoot!

Masconivich Shooter

⅓ part brandy
⅓ part Courvoisier cognac
⅓ part Hiram Walker Cointreau
Lemon wheel
Sugar to coat lemon wheel
Instant coffee to coat lemon wheel

Remove the rind from the lemon wheel. Coat one side of the lemon wheel with sugar and the other side with instant coffee. Bite the wheel and shoot the drink! Serve in a pony or cordial glass.

Matador

1 oz. Licor 43
1 oz. Jägermeister, cold

Serve in a snifter glass.

 ALFONSO BUCETA • STROUDSBURG, PA

Mattapoo

1 oz. Smirnoff vodka
½ oz. Midori melon liqueur
¼ oz. grapefruit juice
¼ oz. pineapple juice

Shake with ice, and strain into a shot glass.

Maureen's Jellybean

1 ½ oz. Echte Kroatzbeere blackberry
  liqueur
⅛ oz. ouzo

Float ouzo on top of liqueur.

McGuido

1 oz. amaretto
1 oz. Irish Mist liqueur

Shake with ice, and strain into a chilled shot
glass.

 JOHN CISCO • CORNERSTONE CAFE •
PATCHOGUE, NY

M.D. Pepper

1 part amaretto
1 part Bacardi 151 rum
1 part beer

Build.

Me and My Gal

1 part cranberry juice
1 part Galliano
1 part Midori melon liqueur

Meat & Potatoes

2 oz. Teton Glacier potato vodka, chilled
Slice pepperoni or dry sausage for garnish

Fill a shot glass with the cold vodka. Garnish with
a generous slice of pepperoni or dry sausage.

Melon Ball

3 parts pineapple juice
2 parts Midori melon liqueur
1 part Finlandia vodka

Shake with ice, and strain into a shot glass.

Melon Ball #2

¾ oz. Midori melon liqueur
½ oz. Absolut vodka
¼ oz. orange juice
¼ oz. pineapple juice

Shake with ice, and strain into a shot glass.

Melon Snowball

¾ oz. Frïs vodka
¾ oz. Midori melon liqueur
½ oz. pineapple juice
Dash half-and-half

Serve with crushed ice in a shot glass.

Melonnium or Shannon's Sweet (Sur)prize

½ oz. DeKuyper Watermelon Pucker
   schnapps
½ oz. Malibu rum
½ oz. Midori melon liqueur
¼ oz. pineapple juice
Splash 7-Up

 SHANNON FRENZEN • GENOA, NE

Memphis Belle

1 oz. Baileys Irish cream
1 oz. Southern Comfort

Build.

Menta B

1 oz. brandy
½ oz. Fernet Branca Menta

Serve as a shot.

Mexican Berry

1 part Chambord
1 part Jose Cuervo tequila

Build.

Mexican Chiller

¾ oz. tequila
¼ oz. Clamato juice
Drop Tabasco

Mexican Flag

½ oz. grenadine
½ oz. green crème de menthe
½ oz. Baileys Irish cream

Build.

Mexican Flag #2

½ oz. sloe gin
½ oz. vodka
½ oz. Midori melon liqueur

Pour sloe gin into a shot glass. Float vodka on top, then Midori on top of that.

Mexican Grandberry

1 oz. Jose Cuervo tequila
½ oz. sweet and sour mix
¼ oz. Chambord
¼ oz. Grand Marnier

Shake with ice, and strain into a shot glass.

Mexican Missile

¾ oz. Jose Cuervo tequila
¾ oz. green Chartreuse liqueur
Dash Tabasco

Combine tequila and Chartreuse in a shot glass. Add a dash of Tabasco to season.

Midnight Sun

1 ¼ oz. Finlandia cranberry vodka
½ oz. Kahlúa

Shake with ice, and strain into a shot glass.

Midori Kamikaze

3 parts Midori melon liqueur
1 part Rose's lime juice
Splash Cointreau

Shake with ice, and serve.

Mikey Mike

1 oz. Malibu rum
½ oz. Chambord
½ oz. DeKuyper Peachtree schnapps
¼ oz. orange juice
¼ oz. pineapple juice

 MICHAEL MANOSH • PROVIDENCE, RI

Miles of Smiles

1 part Seagram's V.O. whiskey
1 part Disaronno amaretto
1 part Rumple Minze peppermint schnapps

Build.

Milk of Amnesia

1 part Baileys Irish cream
1 part Jägermeister

Build.

Milky Way

1 oz. whipped cream
½ oz. amaretto
½ oz. dark crème de cacao

Shake with ice, and strain into a shot glass.

Milky Way #2

½ oz. Kahlúa
½ oz. Smirnoff vodka
¼ oz. dark crème de cacao
Whipped cream to top

Shake with ice, and strain into a shot glass. Top
with whipped cream.

Milky Way #3

¾ oz. Kahlúa
½ oz. Baileys Irish cream
½ oz. Tuaca
Dash half-and-half

 TODD OSTERHOUSE • AUSTIN, TX

Milwaukee River

½ oz. Kahlúa
½ oz. blue curaçao
½ oz. Baileys Irish cream

Build.

Mind Collapse

½ oz. Hiram Walker peppermint schnapps
½ oz. Jägermeister
½ oz. Jameson Irish whiskey

Shake with ice, and strain into a shot glass.

Mind Eraser

1 part Stolichnaya vodka
1 part Kahlúa
1 part club soda

Build.

Mini Margarita

1 part Cointreau
1 part Sauza tequila
Lime wedge for garnish

Serve in a test tube and garnish with a lime wedge.

Mini Martini

⅓ oz. French vermouth
⅓ oz. gin
⅓ oz. Italian vermouth
4 dashes Absente absinthe

Shake with ice, and strain into a shot glass.

 JOHN F. PFLUGH • ROLLIOUX, CA

Mint-2-Lips

½ oz. Baileys Irish cream
½ oz. crème de cacao
¼ oz. green crème de menthe
¼ oz. milk
¼ oz. rum

Shake with ice, and strain into a shot glass.

 TERI BLINSON • TEMPE, AZ

Mint Julep

1 oz. Maker's Mark bourbon
½ oz. Hiram Walker green crème de menthe

Build.

Misdemeanor

½ oz. DeKuyper Buttershots schnapps
½ oz. Crown Royal whiskey

Build.

 BIG KEL • PEORIA, IL

Missing Link

1 part Romana Black sambuca
1 part Rumple Minze peppermint schnapps
1 part Jägermeister

Build.

 KAM S. YU • CHOPSTICKS RESTAURANT •
LEOMINSTER, MA

Mission Accomplished

2 oz. Smirnoff vodka
½ oz. Cointreau
¼ oz. Rose's lime juice
Dash grenadine

Shake with ice, and strain into a shot glass.
Serves two.

The Mission Impossible (Should You Accept It)

½ oz. Grande Absente absinthe
½ oz. tequila

Serve in a shot glass. This drink should self-destruct in 5 seconds....

Misty Dew

1 oz. Irish Mist liqueur
1 oz. Tullamore Dew Irish whiskey

Build.

Mona's Man

½ oz. Disaronno amaretto
½ oz. Malibu rum
½ oz. Mount Gay rum
¼ oz. orange juice
¼ oz. pineapple juice

Shake with ice, and strain into a shot glass.

Monkey Gland

1 oz. Bombay gin
¼ oz. Benedictine brandy
Dash grenadine
Dash orange juice

Shake with ice, and strain into a shot glass.

Monkey Poop

¾ oz. crème de banana
¾ oz. vodka
Splash orange juice
Splash pineapple juice
Dash Rose's lime juice

Shake with ice, and strain into a shot glass.

Monkey See, Monkey Do

3 parts orange juice
1 part Baileys Irish cream
1 part banana liqueur
1 part Myers's Original dark rum

Shake with ice, and strain into a shot glass.

Monkey Wrench

1 oz. Bacardi rum
½ oz. orange juice
½ oz. sweet and sour mix
Dash grenadine

Shake the first three ingredients with ice and strain into a shot glass. Float a dash of grenadine on top.

Monkey's Lunch

¾ oz. Kahlúa
½ oz. crème de banana
½ oz. Myers's rum cream liqueur

Build.

Monk's Slide

1 part Frangelico
1 part Tuaca liqueur
1 part Baileys Irish cream

Build.

 JENNIFER MILLS • PESCATORE ITALIAN
RESTAURANT • HILO, HI

Monsoon

¼ oz. Kahlúa
¼ oz. Hiram Walker amaretto
¼ oz. Frïs vodka
¼ oz. Carolans Irish cream
¼ oz. Frangelico

Build.

Moody Blue

⅓ oz. amaretto
⅓ oz. blueberry schnapps
⅓ oz. gin

Build.

Morgan's Jolly Roger

1 part Captain Morgan rum
1 part cinnamon schnapps

Build.

Morgan's Wench

1 part Captain Morgan rum
1 part Disaronno amaretto
Dark crème de cacao to float

Build the first two ingredients. Float crème de cacao on top.

Mother Load

1 part Absolut vodka
1 part Leroux blackberry brandy
1 part Malibu rum

Build.

 VANNIE NESS • GORDY'S TAVERN • KENOSHA, WI

Mother's Milk

1 part amaretto
1 part Baileys Irish cream
1 part Grand Marnier
1 part Kahlúa
1 part light rum
1 part Southern Comfort

Shake with ice, and strain into a shot glass.

 ALVAH L. KNAPP • THE WEST END HOTEL INC. • HAMBURG, NY

Motor Oil

½ oz. DeKuyper Butตershots schnapps
½ oz. DeKuyper Hot Damn! cinnamon
    schnapps
½ oz. Jägermeister

Combine in a shaker with ice and strain into a
shot glass.

Mounds Bar

1 part Baileys Irish cream
1 part dark crème de cacao
1 part Malibu rum
1 part half-and-half (optional)

For extra chocolate flavor, try adding Mozart chocolate liqueur to taste.

Mr. Wilson

¾ oz. apple schnapps
¾ oz. cranberry juice
¾ oz. Malibu rum
¾ oz. orange juice

Shake with ice, and strain into a shot glass.

Mud Slide

1 part Frïs vodka
1 part Kahlúa
1 part Carolans Irish cream

Build. Add Hiram Walker hazelnut liqueur and it's called a Mississippi Mud Pie.

Mustang Sally

1 oz. Absolut vodka
1 oz. Malibu rum
¼ oz. cranberry juice
¼ oz. orange juice

 HOLLY BASKY • DENVER, CO

My Sister, the Doctor, That's Kept in the Basement

¾ oz. Tequila Rose
½ oz. Dr. McGillicuddy's vanilla schnapps
½ oz. Jägermeister

Build.

 RON VILLA • THE BREAK ROOM LOUNGE • MAUMEE, OH

Mystery Madness

1 oz. Bacardi rum
½ oz. blue curaçao
Splash sweet and sour mix

 KIMBERLY PICAZIO • UNCASVILLE, CT

Naked Barbie Doll

1 oz. Malibu rum
½ oz. Bols strawberry liqueur
Pineapple juice

 MARTY WAATT • ATLANTIC CITY, NJ

Naked Politician

1 part Bacardi rum
1 part Captain Morgan rum
1 part Malibu rum
1 part Myers's rum
Splash banana liqueur
Splash orange juice
Splash pineapple juice
Dash grenadine

 MICHAEL MORIN • BOSTON, MA

Napalm Bomb

¾ oz. Chambord
¾ oz. Smirnoff vodka
½ oz. pineapple juice

Shake with ice, and strain into a shot glass.

Nashville Shooter

1 ½ oz. Absolut vodka
Splash cranberry juice
Splash sweet and sour mix
½ splash Rose's lime juice

Shake with ice, and strain into a shot glass.

Nasty Lori

1 part Jose Cuervo tequila
1 part peach schnapps
1 part pineapple juice

Shake with ice, and strain into a shot glass.

 LORI A. MARTIN • FORT DICK, CA

Neapolitan

1 part dark crème de cacao
1 part Dr. McGillicuddy's vanilla schnapps
1 part Tequila Rose to top

Layer the first two ingredients in a shot glass.
Top with Tequila Rose.

 MICKEY THORNTON • WEST COVINA, CA

Negroni Shooter

1 part Bombay gin
1 part Campari
1 part sweet vermouth
Splash club soda

Build.

Neon Cactus

2 oz. Rose's lime juice
1 oz. DeKuyper cactus juice liqueur

Shake with ice, and strain into a shot glass.

Nepa Shooter

½ oz. Absolut Kurant vodka
½ oz. Malibu rum
½ oz. pineapple juice
½ oz. Stolichnaya Ohranj vodka
¼ oz. Cointreau
Splash Chambord

 ROBERT ROTHLEIN • ST. PETERSBURG, FL

Nero's Delight

1 part Romana sambuca
1 part Baileys Irish cream

Layer in a shot glass.

Nettie's Knockout

1 ½ oz. Midori melon liqueur
½ oz. Cointreau
Splash Squirt

 FRONTIER CITY SALOON • CHARLOTTE, MI

Neutron Blaster

½ oz. Baileys Irish cream
½ oz. Disaronno amaretto
½ oz. Grand Marnier
½ oz. Kahlúa

Shake with ice, and strain into a shot glass.

New York Slammer

½ oz. amaretto
½ oz. orange juice
½ oz. Southern Comfort
¼ oz. Cointreau
¼ oz. sloe gin

Shake with ice, and strain into a shot glass.

Night Moves

¼ oz. Baileys Irish cream
¼ oz. Captain Morgan rum
¼ oz. DeKuyper Buttershots schnapps
¼ oz. Kahlúa
¼ oz. vanilla schnapps

 PAM HUNTER • FRANKFORT, IN

Nighthawk

1 oz. Myers's rum
1 oz. Rumple Minze peppermint schnapps

Build.

Nightmare Shooter

¾ oz. Bombay gin
¾ oz. Dubonnet
¼ oz. cherry brandy
Splash orange juice

Shake with ice, and strain into a shot glass.

Ninety-Nine (99)

1 oz. Carolans Irish cream
1 oz. Tullamore Dew Irish whiskey

Stir with ice, and serve straight up.

Ninja

¾ oz. Kahlúa
½ oz. Midori melon liqueur
¾ oz. Frangelico

Build.

Ninja Turtle

1 oz. pineapple juice
1 oz. Southern Comfort
½ oz. Midori melon liqueur
½ oz. sweet and sour mix

Shake with ice, and strain into a shot glass.

Northern Exposure

1 part Malibu rum
1 part Canadian Mist whisky

Build.

 SARAJ AMANN • EVANSVILLE, WI

Not

½ oz. Opal Nera black sambuca
½ oz. ouzo
½ oz. tequila

Build.

 VANNIE NESS • GORDY'S BAR • KENOSHA, WI

Notorious

2 ½ oz. Jose Cuervo Silver tequila

Serve straight up in a cognac snifter.

 R. FOLEY • LIBERTY CORNER, NJ

Nuclear Accelerator

½ oz. Frïs vodka
½ oz. Hiram Walker peppermint schnapps
½ oz. Grand Marnier

Build.

Nuclear Holocaust

1 part banana schnapps
1 part blue curaçao
1 part cranberry juice
1 part Mount Gay rum
1 part peach schnapps

Shake with ice, and strain into a shot glass.

 P.J. JOELTING • KANSAS CITY, MO

Nude Bomb

½ oz. Kahlúa
½ oz. banana liqueur
½ oz. amaretto

Layer in order in a 1½-oz. shot glass and serve.

 STAN GORANOFF • HARWOOD HEIGHTS, IL

Numero Uno

1 oz. Sauza Conmemorativo tequila
½ oz. Hiram Walker Cointreau

Shake with ice, and strain into a shot glass.

Nut Cracker

1 part Frangelico
1 part Myers's rum cream liqueur
1 part Rumple Minze peppermint schnapps

Shake with ice, and strain into a shot glass.

Nut Cracker #2

¾ oz. Stolichnaya vodka
¾ oz. Frangelico
½ oz. half-and-half

Build.

Nut 'N Holli

¼ oz. Carolans Irish cream
¼ oz. Frangelico
¼ oz. Irish Mist liqueur

Shake. Serve straight up in a shot glass.

Nut Slammer

½ oz. milk or half-and-half
¼ oz. Absolut vodka
¼ oz. amaretto
¼ oz. Frangelico
¼ oz. Kahlúa

Nuts & Berries

½ oz. Baileys Irish cream
½ oz. Chambord
½ oz. Frangelico
½ oz. half-and-half

Shake with ice, and strain into a shot glass.

Nutty Blonde Goes Bananas

1 oz. banana liqueur
½ oz. Malibu rum
½ oz. pineapple juice
½ oz. Sierra Mist

 KATIE FLYNN • DES MOINES, WA

Nutty Irishman

½ oz. Frangelico
½ oz. Baileys Irish cream

Build.

Nutty Jamaican

1 oz. Myers's rum cream liqueur
¾ oz. Frangelico

Shake with ice, and strain into a shot glass.

Nutty Professor

½ oz. Baileys Irish cream
½ oz. Frangelico
½ oz. Grand Marnier

Stir and strain into a shot glass.

Nutty Scotsman

1 oz. amaretto
1 oz. Drambuie

Layer.

 ISLA WOTHERSPOON • WILSONVILLE, OR

Nutty Surfer

2 parts Malibu rum
1 part Frangelico
1 part half-and-half

Shake with ice, and strain into a shot glass.

Oatmeal Cookie

1 oz. Baileys Irish cream
1 oz. Frangelico
¼ oz. Goldschläger

Shake with ice, and strain into a shot glass.

Oatmeal Cookie #2

¼ part Baileys Irish cream
¼ part butterscotch schnapps
¼ part Jägermeister
¼ part Kahlúa

Shake with ice, and strain into a shot glass.

O-Bomb

1 oz. orange juice
1 oz. Red Bull
1 shot Skyy Infusions Citrus vodka, chilled

Fill a pint glass with the first two ingredients.
Drop vodka shot into the glass.

 MICHELLE KRYWKO • THE HIDEOUT •
CLAWSON, MI

O'Casey Scotch Terrier

1 part Baileys Irish cream
1 part J&B scotch whisky

Build.

Ocean Breeze

½ oz. cranberry juice
¾ oz. Chambord
¾ oz. Cointreau

Shake with ice, and strain into a shot glass.

Oh My Gosh

1 oz. DeKuyper Peachtree schnapps
1 oz. Disaronno amaretto

Stir with ice, and strain into a shot glass.

Oil Slick

¾ oz. Rumple Minze peppermint schnapps
¾ oz. Jägermeister

Build.

Oil Slick #2

¾ oz. Rumple Minze peppermint schnapps
¾ oz. Jim Beam bourbon

Build.

Oil Slick #3

1 oz. Der Lachs Original Danziger goldwasser
⅛ oz. black sambuca

Serve in a chilled shot glass.

Old Glory

⅓ oz. Dr. McGillicuddy's Mentholmint
    schnapps
⅓ oz. grenadine
⅓ oz. blue curaçao

Build.

Old Lay

1 ¼ oz. Jose Cuervo Gold tequila
¾ oz. Cointreau
¾ oz. Rose's lime juice
Dash grenadine

Shake with ice, and strain into a shot glass.

One Potato

2 oz. Teton Glacier potato vodka

Serve chilled in a shot glass.

Orangatang

1 part Absolut vodka
1 part Midori melon liqueur
1 part orange juice
1 part Southern Comfort

Blend and chill, serve in a shot glass.

 KIM • TOMMY'S MARDI GRAS • STONE PARK, IL

Orange Bush

1 oz. orange juice
½ oz. Grand Marnier
¼ oz. Smirnoff vodka

Shake with ice, and strain into a shot glass.

Orange Crush

1 oz. Absolut vodka
½ oz. Cointreau
½ oz. orange juice
Dash 7-Up

Shake with ice, and strain into a shot glass. Top with 7-Up.

Orange Julius

3 oz. beer
2 oz. orange juice
1 oz. Disaronno amaretto

Serve in a frosted shot glass. Serves two.

 MISSI LANGSTON • SAN ANTONIO, TX

Orange Lifesaver

¾ oz. Absolut Mandrin vodka, Stolichnaya
   Ohranj vodka, or Bacardi O rum
½ oz. cranberry juice
½ oz. pineapple juice
½ oz. triple sec

Shake with ice, and strain into a shot glass.

 JASON DUNSTONE • TGI FRIDAY'S • DESTIN, FL

Oreo Cookie

1 part half-and-half
1 part Kahlúa
1 part Romana Black sambuca

Shake with ice, and strain into a shot glass.

Orgasm

1 part Baileys Irish cream
1 part Disaronno amaretto
1 part Kahlúa

Shake with ice, and strain into a shot glass.

Orgasm #2

1 ½ oz. Southern Comfort
¾ oz. pineapple juice or orange juice
½ oz. amaretto

Shake with ice, and strain into a shot glass.

Orgasm #3

¾ oz. peppermint schnapps
½ oz. Myers's rum cream liqueur

Build.

Orgasm #4

¾ oz. Baileys Irish cream
¾ oz. Disaronno amaretto

Shake with ice, and strain into a shot glass.

Oyster from Hell

1 oyster, raw
Jose Cuervo tequila to fill
3 dashes Tabasco

In a shot glass place one raw oyster, fill with
tequila and three dashes of Tabasco.

 MICHAEL BURRELL • ELEGANT BUNS RESTAURANT
AND BAR • SAN JOSE, CA

Oyster Shooter

2 oysters, raw
¾ shot Absolut vodka
2 splashes Bloody Mary mix
Lemon wedge for garnish

Place oysters in a pony or cordial glass. Pour
in vodka and Bloody Mary mix. Bite the lemon
wedge and shoot.

Oyster Shooter #2 (a.k.a. Slimer)

1 oyster, raw
1 shot Absolut Peppar vodka
Spoonful horseradish
Dash cocktail sauce

Mix in a shooter glass and slide it down!

Panama Jack

1 ¼ oz. Yukon Jack whiskey
¾ oz. pineapple juice
Splash club soda

Shake the first two ingredients with ice and strain into a shot glass. Top with a splash of soda.

Panama Red

1 oz. Jose Cuervo Gold tequila
¼ oz. Cointreau
¼ oz. grenadine
¼ oz. sweet and sour mix

Shake with ice, and strain into a shot glass.

Pancho Villa

½ oz. crème de almond
½ oz. Jose Cuervo tequila
½ oz. Bacardi 151 rum

Layer crème de almond and tequila in a shot glass. Float rum on top.

Panther

¾ oz. peach brandy
¾ oz. white crème de menthe

Shake with ice, and strain into a shot glass.

Panty Burner

1 part Disaronno amaretto
1 part Frangelico
1 part Kahlúa

Stir with ice, and strain into a shot glass.

Paradise

1 ½ oz. Puerto Rican rum
½ oz. Hiram Walker apricot brandy

Build.

 JAMIE WILSON • LANGLEY, WA

Paramedic

1 shot Absolut vodka
4 drops Tabasco

Build.

 LISA SWITZER • KNOX AMERICAN LEGION •
KNOX, PA

Paranoia

1 oz. Hiram Walker amaretto
½ oz. orange juice

Shake with ice, and strain into a shot glass.

Parisian Blonde

¾ oz. Bacardi rum
¾ oz. Cointreau
¾ oz. Myers's Original dark rum

Shake with ice, and strain into a shot glass.

Passion Cream

1 oz. half-and-half
1 oz. white crème de cacao

Shake with ice, and strain into a shot glass.

Passion Potion

1 oz. Agavero tequila liqueur
1 oz. Jose Cuervo 1800 tequila
Maraschino cherry

Serve in a shot glass over ice.

Patriot

½ oz. Galliano
½ oz. Kahlúa
½ oz. Baileys Irish cream

Carefully float one ingredient over the other in
the order above to form layers. Do not stir.

Peace in Ireland

½ oz. Carolans Irish cream
½ oz. Irish Mist liqueur or Tullamore Dew
   Irish whiskey

Shake with ice, and strain into a shot glass.

Peach Almond Shake

1 oz. amaretto
½ oz. half-and-half
½ oz. peach schnapps

Shake with ice, and strain into a shot glass.

Peach Bunny

¾ oz. DeKuyper Peachtree schnapps
¾ oz. light cream
¾ oz. white crème de cacao

Shake with ice, and strain into a cordial glass.

Peach Pirate

¾ oz. Hiram Walker peach schnapps
½ oz. Bacardi rum

Build.

Peach Pit

1 part apple schnapps
1 part peach schnapps

Stir with ice, and strain into a shot glass.

Peach Preparation

1 oz. Bacardi 151 rum
1 oz. peach schnapps

Shake with ice, and strain into a shot glass.

Peach Tart

1 oz. DeKuyper Peachtree schnapps
½ oz. lime juice

Stir with ice, and strain into a shot glass.

Peaches and Cream

¾ oz. peach schnapps
½ oz. half-and-half
Dash Bacardi 151 rum

Shake with ice, and strain into a shot glass.

Peachmeister

1 shot Jägermeister
Splash DeKuyper Peachtree schnapps

Peanut Butter & Jelly

¾ oz. Chambord
¾ oz. Frangelico

Shake with ice, and strain into a shot glass.

Pear Harbor

1 oz. Suntory vodka
¾ oz. pineapple juice
¼ oz. Midori melon liqueur

Shake with ice, and strain into a shot glass.

Pecker Head

⅔ shot Disaronno amaretto
⅔ shot Yukon Jack whiskey
Splash pineapple juice

Shake with ice, and strain into a shot glass.

Pee Wee's Beamer

¾ oz. Malibu rum
¾ oz. Tanqueray Sterling vodka
Orange juice

Shake with ice, and strain into a shot glass.

Penalty Shot

1 oz. Hiram Walker peppermint schnapps
1 oz. Kahlúa

Chill over ice and strain into a shot glass.

 TOM ROCK • BARTENDERS IN THE BURBS •
DEDHAM, MA

Penetrator

1 part Absolut vodka
1 part Galliano
Chilled lemon
Sugar to coat lemon

Pour the first two ingredients into a shooter glass. Cut the lemon and coat it with sugar. Shoot, then bite the lemon.

Pepper Pot

1 ¼ oz. Hiram Walker cinnamon schnapps
Dash Tabasco

Shake with ice, and strain into a shot glass.

Peppermint Banana

¾ oz. crème de banana
½ oz. Rumple Minze peppermint schnapps
¼ oz. Baileys Irish cream

In a shooter glass, combine crème de banana
and peppermint schnapps. Carefully float
Baileys on top.

 GARY ELASS • N. CANTON, OH

Peppermint Patty

1 part dark crème de cacao
1 part Kahlúa
1 part Rumple Minze peppermint schnapps
Splash cream

Shake with ice, and strain into a shot glass.

Peppermint Twist

¾ oz. Stolichnaya vodka
½ oz. Baileys Irish cream
½ oz. Rumple Minze peppermint schnapps

Build.

Perfect Storm

½ oz. Jägermeister
½ oz. Tuaca liqueur
1 can Red Bull

Add the first two ingredients to a shot glass. Fill a pint glass with Red Bull. Drop the shot into the Red Bull.

 JAMES CASON • CORPUS CHRISTI, TX

Pernod Demon

1 ½ oz. Pernod
Lemon wedge
Sugar to coat wedge
Tabasco to coat wedge

Coat the lemon wedge with sugar and Tabasco. Suck the lemon and then shoot Pernod.

Peter's Shot

1 oz. Killepitsch herbal liqueur
1 oz. Teton Glacier potato vodka

 PETER TENNANT • NEW YORK, NY

Pick Me Up Jose

1 oz. Jose Cuervo Especial tequila
½ oz. Captain Morgan rum

Serve in a shot glass.

Pickle Tickle

1 oz. Jose Cuervo Gold tequila
1 oz. pickle juice

Shoot the Cuervo and chase with pickle juice.

Pickleback

2 oz. pickle juice
2 oz. Jameson Irish whiskey

Serve as a shot.

Pile Driver

½ oz. Bacardi 151 rum
½ oz. J&B scotch whisky
½ oz. tequila
Dash Rose's lime juice
Dash grenadine

Chill the first four ingredients over ice and strain into a shot glass. Float grenadine on top.

 MICHAEL KIRSCH • GENEROUS GEORGE'S • ALEXANDRIA, VA

Pineapple Bomb

1 part Disaronno amaretto
1 part pineapple juice
1 part Southern Comfort
Splash club soda (optional)

Add a splash of club soda if you'd like, and suck it up quickly with a straw.

Pineapple Bomb #2

1 oz. Malibu rum
¾ oz. pineapple juice
¼ oz. Bacardi dark rum

Shake with ice, and strain into a shot glass.

Pineapple Bomb #3

1 oz. pineapple juice
¾ oz. Captain Morgan rum
¾ oz. Southern Comfort
½ oz. Disaronno amaretto

Shake with ice, and strain into a shot glass.
Serves two.

Pineapple Upside-Down Cake

1 oz. Finlandia vodka
½ oz. pineapple juice
Whipped cream to top

Serve in a shot glass. Top with whipped cream.

Pink Caddy

¾ oz. Licor 43
¾ oz. Sauza tequila
½ oz. cranberry juice

Shake with ice, and strain into a shot glass.

Pink Cadillac

2 parts Keke Beach key lime liqueur
2 parts pineapple juice
1 part cranberry juice
1 part Mount Gay rum

Shake with ice, and strain into a shot glass.

Pink Cod

1 oz. Jose Cuervo 1800 tequila
¾ oz. sweet and sour mix
¼ oz. Grand Marnier
Splash cranberry juice

Shake with ice, and strain into a shot glass.

Pink Lemonade

1 ½ oz. Absolut Citron vodka
½ oz. cranberry juice
½ oz. sweet and sour mix

Shake with ice, and strain into a shot glass.

Pink Nipple

1 shot Chambord
1 shot Baileys Irish cream
Dash grenadine

Build the first two ingredients, then add grenadine to create a nipple.

Pink Nipple #2

1 ½ oz. Finlandia cranberry vodka
¼ oz. Romana sambuca

Shake with ice, and strain into a shot glass.

Pink Petal

1 part DeKuyper Hot Damn! cinnamon schnapps
1 part Goldschläger

 PAM BENNETT • FISHERS LANDING, NY

Pink Squirrel

1 oz. half-and-half
½ oz. crème de noyaux
½ oz. white crème de cacao

Shake with ice, and strain into a shot glass.

Pirates' Gold

2 parts rum
1 part Goldschläger

Shake with ice, and strain into a shot glass.

 KORIN PRICE • EL RANCHO SALOON •
STEAMBOAT SPRINGS, CO

Pixie Stick

1 part DeKuyper Grape Pucker schnapps
1 part Stolichnaya Ohranj vodka
1 part sweet and sour mix

 KARL DOVER • BIRMINGHAM, AL

Pleading Insanity

½ oz. Myers's Original dark rum
½ oz. Sauza Gold tequila
½ oz. Stolichnaya vodka

Shake with ice, and strain into a shot glass.

Point

¾ oz. Drambuie
¾ oz. white crème de menthe
½ oz. Irish cream

Layer.

Polar Bear

1 oz. half-and-half
½ oz. Stolichnaya vodka
½ oz. white crème de cacao

Shake with ice, and strain into a shot glass.

Polish Red Hair (Cherry Coke)

2 oz. Luksusowa vodka
1 oz. amaretto
1 oz. Rose's lime juice
2 drops grenadine
Coke to fill

Serve in a glass shaker. Put two or three straws in, and drink it down with several friends.

 MISSI LANGSTON • SAN ANTONIO, TX

Ponce Appeal

Shot Bacardi Limón rum
Shot Captain Morgan rum
Splash lemonade
Lemon wedge

Shake with ice, and strain into a shot glass. Rim
with fresh lemon or a squeeze of lemon.

 MICHAEL MILLER & DANIEL BAIER •
CEDAR RAPIDS, IA

Ponce de Limón

Shot Bacardi Limón rum
Shot Captain Morgan rum
Splash cola

 MICHAEL MILLER & DANIEL BAIER •
CEDAR RAPIDS, IA

Popper

1 part Jose Cuervo tequila
1 part champagne

Layer in a rocks glass. Cover the shot and slam it
(gently) on the table. Drink it while it fizzes over.
Use a very durable glass.

Popsicle

2 parts Chambord
2 parts Frangelico
1 part pineapple juice

Shake with ice, and strain into a shot glass.

Portofino

1 shot Tuaca liqueur, chilled
Angostura bitters
Lime wedge
Sugar packet

Take a wedge of lime between your middle finger and thumb. Put two drops of Angostura bitters on the lime. No more, no less. Sprinkle ¼ packet of sugar on the lime. No more, no less. Put the lime in your mouth. Remove the lime from your mouth and drink the shot.

Pot O' Gold

⅔ oz. Goldschläger
½ oz. Baileys Irish cream

Build.

Prairie Fire

1 ½ oz. Jose Cuervo Gold tequila
Dash Tabasco

Fill a shot glass with chilled Cuervo Gold tequila.
Add a dash of Tabasco.

Pretty in Pink

¾ oz. crème de noyaux
¾ oz. Myers's Original dark rum
½ oz. half-and-half

Shake with ice, and strain into a shot glass.

The Princess's Orgasm

½ oz. Absolut vanilla vodka
½ oz. Chambord
½ oz. Red Bull
Splash cranberry juice

Shake with ice, and strain into a shot glass.

 KATHY SOMMER • KATHY'S PLACE •
HONOLULU, HI

Pumpkin Pie

1 part Absolut vodka
1 part apple juice
Dash cinnamon

Shake with ice, and strain into a shot glass.

Pumpkin Smasher

½ oz. orange juice
½ oz. peach schnapps
½ oz. Tuaca liqueur
½ oz. vodka
¼ oz. DeKuyper Hot Damn! cinnamon
    schnapps

 KEN HOOD • PORT ARTHUR, TX

Puppy's Nose

½ oz. Kahlúa
½ oz. Rumple Minze peppermint schnapps
½ oz. Tia Maria
¼ oz. Baileys Irish cream

Shake with ice, and strain into a shot glass.

Purple Haze

¾ oz. Chambord
¾ oz. Stolichnaya vodka
½ oz. cranberry juice or sweet and sour mix

Shake with ice, and strain into a shot glass.

Purple Heart

1 part Absolut Kurant vodka
1 part Chambord
1 part cranberry juice

Shake with ice, and strain into a shot glass.

Purple Hooter

¾ oz. Chambord
¾ oz. Finlandia vodka
½ oz. Rose's sweet and sour mix

Shake with ice, and strain into a shot glass.

Purple Hooter #2

1 oz. vodka
½ oz. Chambord
½ oz. cranberry juice

Shake with ice, and strain into a shot glass.

Purple Nurple

½ oz. tequila
¼ oz. Hiram Walker blue curaçao
¼ oz. Hiram Walker sloe gin
Splash Tabasco

Shake with ice, and strain into a shot glass.

Purple Orchid

1 oz. blackberry brandy
½ oz. half-and-half
½ oz. white crème de cacao

Shake with ice, and strain into a shot glass.

Purple Panther

1 ¼ oz. Finlandia cranberry vodka
Splash blue curaçao

Shake with ice, and strain into a shot glass.

Purple Passion

1 ½ oz. Finlandia cranberry vodka
½ oz. Chambord

Shake with ice, and strain into a shot glass.

Purple Peaches

1 oz. Stolichnaya Peachnik vodka
½ oz. peach schnapps
½ oz. Chambord

Build.

 JENNIFER PORTER • MT. SHASTA, CA

Purple Perfection

½ oz. Absolut Citron vodka
½ oz. Chambord
Splash ginger ale
Splash orange juice
Splash pineapple juice

 PATRICK BILLERMAN • SEA GIRT, NJ

Purple Pirate

½ oz. Captain Morgan rum
½ oz. Chambord
Splash 7-Up

 JOHN DOYLE • PHILADELPHIA, PA

Purple Rain

1 ½ oz. Sobieski vodka
¾ oz. cranberry juice
Splash blue curaçao

Shake with ice, and strain into a shot glass.

 WILLIAM WILSON • SEATTLE, WA

Queen Bee

1 oz. Bafferts gin
1 oz. Fernet Branca

Serve as a shot.

Quick Sand

½ oz. Absolut vodka
½ oz. Kahlúa
½ oz. Original Bartenders Cocktails Hot Sex

Layer in order, the Hot Sex last. It looks like quicksand.

 DEB CHAPMAN • BOB'S SAND BAR •
LIN GROVE, IA

Quick Silver

⅓ oz. white crème de cacao
⅓ oz. peppermint schnapps
⅓ oz. tequila

Build.

Quickie

½ oz. Hiram Walker crème de banana
½ oz. Hiram Walker blackberry brandy
½ oz. Carolans Irish cream

Build.

Racer's Edge

1 oz. Bacardi rum
¼ oz. Hiram Walker crème de menthe
Splash grapefruit juice

Shake with ice, and strain into a shot glass.

Raggedy Andy

1 oz. half-and-half
1 oz. Mozart chocolate liqueur
½ oz. crème de banana

Shake with ice, and strain into a shot glass.

Raggedy Ann

1 oz. half-and-half
1 oz. Mozart chocolate liqueur
½ oz. peppermint schnapps

Shake with ice, and strain into a shot glass.

Raider

⅓ oz. Drambuie
⅓ oz. Baileys Irish cream
⅓ oz. Grand Marnier
⅓ oz. Kahlúa

Build.

Rainbow

½ oz. crème de noyaux
½ oz. Midori melon liqueur
½ oz. white crème de cacao

Build.

Raspberry Brownie

¾ oz. Chambord
¾ oz. Kahlúa
Half-and-half or milk to float

Raspberry Cheesecake

¾ oz. Chambord
¾ oz. Baileys Irish cream
½ oz. half-and-half

Build.

Raspberry Kiss

1 oz. Chambord
1 oz. half-and-half
½ oz. Kahlúa

Shake with ice, and strain into a shot glass.

Raspberry Screamer

1 oz. Absolut vodka
1 oz. Chambord
1 oz. pineapple juice

Shake with ice, and strain into a shot glass.

Raspberry Shooter

2 parts Chambord
1 part Absolut vodka
Splash orange juice

Shake with ice, and strain into a shot glass.

Raspberry Shortcake

1 oz. Chambord
1 oz. Baileys Irish cream

Build.

Rastini

¾ oz. Chambord
¾ oz. Smirnoff vodka
Splash Rose's sweet and sour mix
Splash 7-Up

Shake the first three ingredients with ice and strain into a shot glass. Top with 7-Up.

Rattlesnake

1 part Kahlúa
1 part Baileys Irish cream
1 part dark crème de cacao

Build. Add one part of tequila and it's called a
Mexican Rattlesnake.

Rattlesnake #2

1 oz. Yukon Jack whiskey
½ oz. cherry brandy
Splash sweet and sour mix

Shake with ice, and strain into a shot glass.

Raven Shooter

1 oz. Malibu rum
½ oz. cranberry juice
½ oz. pineapple juice
½ oz. vodka

Shake with ice, and strain into a shot glass.

Razor

¾ oz. Bacardi 151 rum
¾ oz. Disaronno amaretto
¾ oz. Rumple Minze peppermint schnapps

Shake with ice, and strain into a shot glass.

Razz Sugar Pie

2 oz. Bacardi Razz rum, chilled
Lime wedge
Sugar to coat lime wedge

Coat the lime wedge in sugar. Bite the wedge first, then drink.

Real Gold

1 part Stolichnaya vodka
1 part Goldschläger

Build.

Red & White

1 part Schladerer Himbeergeist schnapps
1 part Schladerer Himbeer liqueur
1 raspberry

Layer in a pony glass. Let the raspberry float in the middle.

Red Baron

1 ½ oz. Absolut Kurant
Splash vodka
Splash cranberry juice

Build.

Red Bird Special

1 shot Absolut vodka
3 splashes tomato juice

Build.

Red Death

½ oz. Disaronno amaretto
½ oz. sloe gin
½ oz. Southern Comfort
2 splashes orange juice

Shake with ice, and strain into a shot glass.

Red Devil

½ oz. Absolut vodka
½ oz. Bacardi rum
¼ oz. crème de cassis
¼ oz. Disaronno amaretto
¼ oz. Southern Comfort
½ splash sweet and sour mix

Shake with ice, and serve.

Red Hot

1 ¼ oz. cinnamon schnapps
Few drops Tabasco

Build.

Red Hot #2

½ oz. Goldschläger
1 oz. Stolichnaya vodka
Dash Tabasco

Build.

Red Lobster

½ oz. Chambord
½ oz. Crown Royal whiskey
½ oz. amaretto
Splash cranberry juice

Build.

 DAREK DOHY • HARD ROCK CAFÉ •
SAN DIEGO, CA

Red October

1 oz. Stolichnaya vodka
½ oz. Midori melon liqueur
½ oz. orange juice
½ oz. sloe gin
Splash sweet and sour mix

Chill over ice and strain into a shot glass.

 DAVID WHYNOT • GILLARY'S • BRISTOL, RI

Red Panties

2 oz. orange juice
1 oz. peach schnapps
1 oz. Smirnoff vodka
½ oz. grenadine

Shake with ice, and strain into a shot glass.

Red Roman

2 oz. Fernet Branca
1 oz. Seagram's vodka
Dash grenadine

Stir. Serve on the rocks.

Red Rum

½ oz. Myers's Original dark rum
½ oz. Southern Comfort
Splash cranberry juice
Splash grenadine
Splash Jack Daniel's whiskey

Shake with ice, and strain into a shot glass. Take one sip, spell the name backward, and the rest is self-explanatory.

 STACEY WILSON • G & M'S RESTAURANT • BALTIMORE, MD

Red Russian

1 oz. Stolichnaya vodka
½ oz. grapefruit juice
½ oz. pineapple juice
Dash grenadine

Shake the first three ingredients with ice and strain into a shot glass. Float grenadine on top.

Red Snapper

½ oz. amaretto
½ oz. Crown Royal whiskey
½ oz. cranberry juice

Build.

Red Tide

⅓ oz. cranberry juice
⅓ oz. Red Bull
⅓ oz. vodka

 MATTHEW JORDAN • DESTIN, FL

Red Whistle

1 ¼ oz. Finlandia cranberry vodka
⅛ oz. Rumple Minze peppermint schnapps
¼ oz. Cointreau

Build. Serve in a test tube.

Red-Eyed Smiley Face

½ oz. Absolut Citron vodka
½ oz. sweet and sour mix
½ oz. Tuaca liqueur
¼ oz. chambord
Splash 7-Up

Regmeister

¾ oz. Southern Comfort
¾ oz. crème de noyaux
½ oz. 7-Up

Build first two ingredients. Top with 7-Up.

Revolution

Dash grenadine
1 oz. ouzo
½ oz. Galliano

Layer in the order listed.

Rhett Butler

1 oz. Southern Comfort
½ oz. Cointreau
½ splash Rose's lime juice
½ splash sweet and sour mix

Shake with ice, and strain into a shot glass.

Rigor Mortis

1 oz. vodka
½ oz. orange juice
½ oz. pineapple juice
¼ oz. amaretto

Shake with ice, and strain into a shot glass.

River Runner

1 ½ oz. Absolut Kurant vodka
¼ oz. blue curaçao
¼ oz. pineapple juice
¼ oz. sweet and sour mix

Shake with ice, and strain into a shot glass.

Roadrunner

½ oz. Grand Marnier
½ oz. Kahlúa

Shake with ice, and strain into a shot glass.

Rock Lobster

1 part white crème de cacao
1 part Baileys Irish cream
Splash Goldschläger

Build.

Rocket Fuel

¾ oz. Rumple Minze peppermint schnapps
½ oz. Bacardi 151 rum

Build.

Rocky Mountain

1 oz. Disaronno amaretto
1 oz. Southern Comfort
½ oz. lime juice

Shake with ice, and strain into a shot glass.

Rocky Road

½ oz. Baileys Irish cream
½ oz. Disaronno amaretto
½ oz. Wild Turkey bourbon

Combine amaretto and Baileys with ice. Shake and strain. Float bourbon on top.

Rolling Blackout

¾ oz. Bacardi 151 rum
¾ oz. Midori melon liqueur
Splash Ocean Spray cranberry juice cocktail

Shake and serve chilled as a shooter.

 NEIL GRUNIG • LOS ANGELES, CA

Roman Candle

1 oz. anisette
½ oz. Galliano
½ oz. orange juice
Dash grenadine

Shake with ice, and strain into a shot glass.

Roman Martini

1 ½ oz. Bombay gin
½ oz. Romana sambuca

Shake with ice, and strain into a shot glass.

Roo-Kon

¾ oz. Yukon Jack whiskey
¼ oz. root beer schnapps

Build.

 JOHN FAZIO • PITTSBURGH, PA

Root Beer Float

2 parts DeKuyper Ragin' Root Beer Burst
    schnapps
1 part Baileys Irish cream
Maraschino cherry for garnish

Make in a test tube. Fill the tube three-quarters
full with root beer schnapps and top with Baileys.
Garnish the tube with a cherry.

Root Beer Float #2

¾ oz. Galliano
¾ oz. Kahlúa
Splash cola
Splash half-and-half

Stir with ice, and strain into a shot glass.

Root Beer Shooter

1 oz. Kahlúa
½ oz. Galliano
Cola to top

Shake the first two ingredients with ice and strain into a shot glass. Top with cola.

Root Canal

1 part Galliano
1 part root beer schnapps

Root Canal #2

¾ oz. Nassau Royale liqueur
¾ oz. root beer schnapps

 BILL BONA • CELEBRATION, FL

Rotten Apple

1 oz. Shakka Apple liqueur
½ oz. Jägermeister

Shake with ice, and strain into a chilled shot glass.

 CHRIS LESCKOWICZ • SHAKKA2ME.COM

Rowdy Dog Wade

1 ½ oz. Jose Cuervo Gold tequila
Juice of ½ lime
Splash of Rose's lime juice

Squeeze the lime into a shaker, add the lime juice and tequila. Shake vigorously.

 ROGER WOLFE • CUJO'S SPORTS BAR & GRILL

Ruby Ridge

1 oz. Southern Comfort
½ oz. amaretto
½ oz. sweet and sour mix
Splash cranberry juice and 7-Up

 BRIAN PSENCIK • AUSTIN, TX

Ruby Slippers

1 part Finlandia cranberry vodka
1 part Goldschläger

Build.

Rum Runner

1 part Bacardi dark rum
1 part Bacardi rum
1 part blackberry brandy
1 part crème de banana
1 part Malibu rum
Orange juice to taste
Sweet and sour mix to taste
Dash grenadine

Shake with ice, and strain into a shot glass.

Rumple Meister

½ oz. Jägermeister
½ oz. Rumple Minze peppermint schnapps

Serve chilled.

Rumpled Rose

¾ shot Rumple Minze peppermint
   schnapps, chilled
½ shot Tequila Rose, chilled

Layer in a frozen shot glass.

Runyan

1 part vodka
1 part Chambord
Splash grape Kool-Aid

Build.

 JOE WITTERS • JOE'S BAR •
COLORADO SPRINGS, CO

Runyan #2

1 part vodka
1 part Chambord
Splash sweet and sour mix

Build.

 CHARLENE WITTEN • COLORADO SPRINGS, CO

Rush Hour

⅓ oz. Kahlúa
⅓ oz. sambuca
⅓ oz. Baileys Irish cream

Build.

Russian Branca

1 oz. Fernet Branca
1 oz. Seagram's vodka

Serve as a shot.

Russian Defect

1 oz. Stolichnaya vodka
½ oz. Rumple Minze peppermint schnapps

Build.

Russian Quaalude

⅓ shot Baileys Irish cream
⅓ shot Frangelico
⅓ shot Stolichnaya vodka

Shake with ice, and strain into a shot glass.

Russian Roulette

½ oz. Galliano, chilled
½ oz. Stolichnaya vodka, chilled
Splash Bacardi 151 rum
Lemon slice
Sugar to coat lemon

Place a sugared lemon slice on a shot glass. Pour a splash of rum, bite the lemon, and do the shot.

Rusted Throat

½ oz. Bacardi 151 rum
½ oz. Bacardi rum
½ oz. KeKe Beach
½ oz. Tropicana orange juice

Shake with ice, and strain into a shot glass.

 RORY L. CHATMAN • NORFOLK, VA

Rusty Nail Shooter

1 part Drambuie
1 part J&B scotch whisky

Build.

Safe Sex on the Beach

1 oz. orange juice
¾ oz. Chambord
¾ oz. peach schnapps

Shake with ice, and strain into a shot glass.

Saint Moritz

1 ¼ oz. Chambord
Half-and-half to float

Pour the Chambord into a glass. Float half-and-half on top.

Salmon Run

1 oz. Jose Cuervo tequila
1 oz. tomato juice
1 oz. orange juice

Serve as three consecutive shots in three glasses.

 DENNIS (DJ) JOHNSON • SHERIDAN, WY

Sambuca

2 oz. sambuca
3 coffee beans for garnish

Sambuca Slide

1 oz. Romana sambuca
½ oz. light cream
½ oz. Stolichnaya vodka

Shake with ice, and strain into a shot glass.

Sambuca Surprise

½ oz. Romana sambuca
½ oz. white crème de menthe
½ oz. white crème de cacao

Build.

Sand in Your Butt

2 parts pineapple juice
1 part Midori melon liqueur
1 part Southern Comfort

Shake with ice, and strain into a shot glass.

Sand Slide

½ oz. Carolans Irish cream
½ oz. Frïs vodka
½ oz. Kahlúa

Shake with ice, and strain into a shot glass.

Sandblaster

½ oz. Jägermeister
¼ oz. C.J. Wray dry rum
½ oz. cola
Squeeze lime wedge

Build.

 JASON NAKAGAWA • TONY ROMA'S •
WESTRIDGE, HI

Santa Sobieski

1 ½ oz. Sobieski vodka
1 oz. Marie Brizard green crème de menthe
Maraschino cherry for garnish

Layer the first two ingredients in a shot glass.
Top with a maraschino cherry.

Saratoga Trunk

1 oz. Tia Maria
1 oz. Tuaca liqueur
½ oz. Hiram Walker cinnamon schnapps

Layer the ingredients in the order listed, and
float cinnamon schnapps on top.

Say Sobieski

2 oz. Sobieski vodka
Squirt lemon or lime juice

Serve in a shot glass and say "Sobieski!"

 WILLIAM FREDRIC • DURHAM, NC • DESTIN, FL

Scarlett O'Hara Shooter

1 oz. Southern Comfort
½ splash grenadine
Splash sweet and sour mix

Shake with ice, and strain into a shot glass.

Schöenauer Apple Schnapps

Schöenauer Apfel schnapps

Serve straight up in a shot glass, chilled, or on the rocks.

Scooter

1 oz. Disaronno amaretto
1 oz. light cream
½ oz. brandy

Shake with ice, and strain into a cordial glass.

Scorpion

1 oz. blackberry brandy
½ oz. vodka

Shake with ice, and strain into a shot glass.

Screamin' Gomez

1 shot tequila
Splash DeKuyper Hot Damn! cinnamon
   schnapps

Screaming Cranapple Shooter

1 oz. Absolut vodka
1 oz. apple schnapps
Splash cranberry juice

Shake with ice, and strain into a shot glass.

Screaming Green Monster

½ oz. Bacardi 151 rum
½ oz. Malibu rum
½ oz. Midori melon liqueur
Splash 7-Up
Splash pineapple juice

 MICHAEL WILLIAMS • HUNTINGTON BEACH, CA

Screaming Multiple Orgasm

½ oz. Baileys Irish cream
½ oz. Cointreau
½ oz. half-and-half
¼ oz. Galliano

Shake with ice, and strain into a shot glass.

Screaming Orgasm

½ oz. Kahlúa
½ oz. Disaronno amaretto
½ oz. Baileys Irish cream
¼ oz. Absolut vodka

Build.

Screaming Orgasm #2

½ oz. Baileys Irish cream
½ oz. Frïs vodka
½ oz. half-and-half
½ oz. Kahlúa

Shake with ice, and strain into a shot glass.

Screaming Orgasm #3

½ oz. half-and-half
½ oz. Kahlúa
½ oz. Stolichnaya vodka
¼ oz. Jose Cuervo tequila
¼ oz. Southern Comfort

Shake with ice, and strain into a shot glass.

Screaming Orgasm against the Wall

¼ oz. Baileys Irish cream
¼ oz. banana liqueur
¼ oz. Disaronno amaretto
¼ oz. Finlandia vodka
¼ oz. Galliano
¼ oz. half-and-half
¼ oz. Kahlúa

Shake with ice, and strain into a shot glass.

Screw

1 shot vodka
1 orange wedge

 SANDI HOWARD • INDIAN WELLS GOLF RESORT •
INDIAN WELLS, CA

Second Childhood

½ oz. Rumple Minze peppermint schnapps
½ oz. Jägermeister
½ oz. Frïs vodka

Build.

Separator

¾ oz. Kahlúa
¾ oz. brandy
½ oz. half-and-half

Build.

Seven Forty Seven (747)

1 part Baileys Irish cream
1 part Frangelico
1 part Kahlúa

Shake with ice, and strain into a shot glass.

Sex in the Parking Lot

½ oz. apple schnapps
½ oz. Chambord
½ oz. Smirnoff vodka

Shake with ice, and strain into a shot glass.

Sex, Lies, and Video Poker

½ oz. amaretto
½ oz. Captain Morgan rum
½ oz. cranberry juice
½ oz. grenadine
½ oz. orange juice
½ oz. pineapple juice
½ oz. Southern Comfort

Shake with ice, and strain into a shot glass.
Makes four.

 JOHN DUGAS, JR. • J&K BAR • NEW ORLEANS, LA

Sex on the Beach

½ oz. Absolut vodka
½ oz. Chambord
½ oz. Midori melon liqueur
Splash pineapple juice

Shake with ice, and strain into a shot glass.

Sex on the Beach #2

¾ oz. Midori melon liqueur
¾ oz. peach schnapps
¼ oz. cranberry juice
¼ oz. orange juice

Shake with ice, and strain into a shot glass.

Sex on the Beach #3

¾ oz. Chambord
½ oz. pineapple juice

Shake with ice, and strain into a shot glass.

Sex on the Beach #4

2 parts cranberry juice
2 parts pineapple juice
1 part Chambord
1 part peach schnapps
1 part Southern Comfort

Shake with ice, and strain into a shot glass.

Sex on the Beach (Southern Style)

½ oz. apple schnapps
½ oz. cranberry juice
½ oz. peach schnapps
½ oz. pineapple juice

Shake with ice, and strain into a shot glass.

Sex on the Lake

¾ oz. crème de banana
¾ oz. dark crème de cacao
½ oz. half-and-half
Dash Bacardi rum

Shake with ice, and strain into a shot glass.

Sex on the Pool Table

½ oz. blueberry schnapps
½ oz. Finlandia vodka
½ oz. Midori melon liqueur
½ oz. orange juice
½ oz. pineapple juice

Shake with ice, and strain into a shot glass.

Sex on the Sidewalk

¾ oz. Chambord
¾ oz. Midori melon liqueur
½ oz. cranberry juice

Shake with ice, and strain into a shot glass.

Sex Up against the Wall

1 part Absolut Kurant vodka
1 part cranberry juice
1 part pineapple juice
1 part sweet and sour mix

Shake with ice, and strain into a shot glass.

Sex with the Captain

½ oz. amaretto
½ oz. Captain Morgan rum
½ oz. peach schnapps
Splash cranberry juice
Splash orange juice

Shake with ice, and strain into a shot glass.

Sexy Rose

½ Tequila Rose
½ Original Bartenders Cocktails Hot Sex

Build.

 JEFF BOWEN • MONROE, WI

Shamrock

½ oz. Carolans Irish cream
½ oz. Midori melon liqueur
½ oz. Tullamore Dew Irish whiskey

Shake and serve as a shot.

Shark Bite Shooter

2 parts orange juice
1 part Myers's Original dark rum
Splash grenadine

Shake with ice, and strain into a shot glass.

Sharpshooter

1 oz. ouzo
1 oz. vodka
Dash Tabasco

Build.

Shazam

½ oz. Jose Cuervo Gold tequila
½ oz. Chambord
½ oz. DeKuyper Peachtree schnapps
4 oz. sweet and sour mix
Splash beer

Build.

 CLAIR BESHEARS • MILFORD, MA

Shipwreck

1 oz. Crown Royal whiskey
¼ oz. Cointreau
¼ oz. cranberry juice
¼ oz. crème de banana
¼ oz. sweet and sour mix

Shake with ice, and strain into a shot glass.

Shock Treatment

1 oz. Grand Marnier
1 oz. Tia Maria

Build.

Shogun Shooter

1 ¼ oz. Frïs vodka
½ oz. Midori melon liqueur

Shake with ice, and strain into a shot glass.

Shot of C

1 ½ oz. Cruzan Citrus rum

Serve in a chilled shot glass.

 GREG CZARNECKI • WEST PALM BEACH, FL

Shot of Ed

1 oz. 151 Bacardi rum
½ oz. Jägermeister
½ oz. Rumple Minze peppermint schnapps

Build.

 SEAN MECHE, JOEY FORET, AND KRIS HEGGELUND
• LAFAYETTE, LA

Shot-O-Happiness

½ oz. Chambord
½ oz. pineapple juice
½ oz. sweet and sour mix
¼ oz. Goldschläger
Splash 7-Up

 JUAN SANDOVAL • SAN ANTONIO, TX

Siberian Express

1 part Dr. McGillicuddy's Mentholmint
    schnapps
1 part half-and-half
1 part Kahlúa
1 part Smirnoff vodka

Shake with ice, and strain into a chilled shot glass.

 DEBBIE BURT • WINTER, WI

Siberian Gold

1 part Goldschläger
1 part Stolichnaya vodka
Splash blue curaçao

Shake with ice, and strain into a shot glass.

 CHRIS "SKIPPY" JONES & GERALD "I'M NOT
RANDY" KIRKMAN • BANANAS • BEAUFORT, SC

Siberian Toolkit

1 oz. Stolichnaya vodka
¼ oz. Baileys Irish cream
¼ oz. Kahlúa
¼ oz. Seagram's V.O. whiskey

Shake with ice, and strain into a shot glass.

Sicilian Kiss

1 part Southern Comfort
1 part Disaronno amaretto
3 parts orange juice
Dash grenadine

Build the first three ingredients. Add grenadine
on top to make a sunset effect.

Sigfried and Branca

1 oz. Fernet Branca
1 oz. Borghetti sambuca

Serve as a shot.

Silk Panties

1 part Stolichnaya vodka
1 part DeKuyper Peachtree schnapps

Build.

Silver Bullet

½ oz. green crème de menthe
½ oz. tequila

Build.

Silver Spider

½ oz. Bacardi rum
½ oz. Smirnoff vodka
½ oz. white crème de menthe
¼ oz. Cointreau

Stir with ice, and strain into a shot glass.

Silver Thread

⅓ oz. crème de banana
⅓ oz. peppermint schnapps
⅓ oz. Baileys Irish cream

Build.

Simply Bonkers

1 oz. Chambord
½ oz. Bacardi rum
½ oz. half-and-half

Shake with ice, and strain into a shot glass.

Sinful Apple

1 part Rimanto potato vodka
¾ part Schöenauer Apfel schnapps

Shake and serve.

Sinfully Hot

¾ oz. tequila
¼ oz. Hiram Walker cinnamon schnapps
Splash Tabasco

Shake with ice, and strain into a shot glass.

Sit Down & Shut Up

⅓ oz. blackberry brandy
⅓ oz. Rumple Minze peppermint schnapps
⅓ oz. Southern Comfort

Shake with ice, and strain into a shot glass.

S.J. Shark's Tooth

1 part Absolut vodka
1 part blue curaçao
1 part piña colada mix

Mix. Serve in a shot glass.

 SANDRA KUKAR • SAN JOSE, CA

Skid Mark

¾ oz. Kahlúa
¾ oz. Baileys Irish cream
¾ oz. Guinness

Build.

 DONNA COLLINS • OCEAN CITY, MD

Skinny Mulligan

⅓ oz. crème de banana
⅓ oz. advocaat
⅓ oz. sloe gin

Build.

Skip and Go Naked

2 parts sweet and sour mix
1 part Beefeater gin
Splash beer

Stir slowly with ice and strain into a shot glass.

Skull Island

1 oz. Jägermeister
¾ oz. DeKuyper Island Punch Pucker
  schnapps
½ oz. sweet and sour mix

Shake with ice, and strain into a shot glass.

 SHANE EVANS • MIDLOTHIAN, VA

Slam Dunk Shooter

1 oz. Monte Alban tequila
Splash club soda
Splash Rose's lime juice

Serve in a pony or cordial glass. Cover the glass
with your hand and rap on the table.

Slammer

1 oz. 7-Up
1 oz. amaretto

Cover with a napkin and slam on the bar. Drink
while the 7-Up is fizzing.

Slice of Apple Pie

1 ¼ oz. Smirnoff vodka
½ oz. apple juice
Cinnamon for garnish

Build the first two ingredients. Sprinkle cinnamon on top.

Slickie Ricky

1 oz. watermelon schnapps
½ oz. Original Bartenders Cocktails Hot
    Sex
Squirt whipped cream

Suck down.

 GINA GEREMIA • NEW HAVEN, CT

Slickster

1 oz. cranberry juice
½ oz. Southern Comfort
¼ oz. 7-Up
¼ oz. peach schnapps

Stir with ice, and strain into a shot glass.

Slimeball

½ cup Midori melon liqueur
1 cup boiling water
Lime Jell-O brand gelatin
½ cup Smirnoff vodka

Add Midori and boiling water to lime Jell-O. Add vodka. Chill to set. Serve in paper soufflé cups. (The Slimeball is a variation of the Jell-O Shot.)

Slippery Baileys

½ oz. Kahlúa
½ oz. crème de banana
½ oz. Baileys Irish cream

Layer in the order listed in a shot glass.

Slippery Chicken

1 part Carolans Irish cream
1 part crème de banana
1 part Grand Marnier

Shake with ice, and strain into a chilled shot glass.

Slippery Lips

1 oz. Absolut vodka
½ oz. Chambord
½ oz. Cointreau
½ oz. cranberry juice
½ oz. orange juice
½ oz. sweet and sour mix

Strain into a shot glass. Serves four.

 DAVID QUIDK • LUKE'S SPORTS SPECTACULAR •
MILWAUKEE, WI

Slippery Nipple

⅔ oz. Romana sambuca
⅓ oz. Baileys Irish cream
Drop grenadine

Build. Add grenadine to the center.

Slippery Nipple #2

⅓ oz. anisette
⅓ oz. peppermint schnapps
⅓ oz. Baileys Irish cream

Build.

Slippery Saddle

½ oz. Finlandia vodka
½ oz. lemon juice
½ oz. Licor 43
½ oz. orange juice

Shake with ice, and strain into a shot glass.

Sloe Slop

1 oz. Stolichnaya vodka
½ oz. sloe gin
¼ oz. 7-Up

Shake the first two ingredients with ice and strain into a shot glass. Top with 7-Up.

Smelly Cat

1 oz. Bacardi Limón
½ oz. peach schnapps
Splash cranberry juice

Build.

 LISA S. ACOSTA • EAST RUTHERFORD, NJ

Smiles

½ oz. Canadian Club whisky
½ oz. Hiram Walker amaretto
½ oz. Hiram Walker peppermint schnapps

Shake with ice, and strain into a shot glass.

Smokey Joe

1 oz. Opal Nera black sambuca
1 oz. Tia Maria

Shake with ice, and strain into a shot glass.

 MARION DEFAZIO • DICKSON CITY, PA

Smooth and Sweet

¾ oz. amaretto
¾ oz. blackberry liqueur
½ oz. pineapple juice

Shake with ice, and strain into a shot glass.

Snake Bite

2 parts Yukon Jack whiskey
1 part Rose's lime juice

Shake with ice, and strain into a shot glass.

Snake Bite #2

1 oz. Jack Daniel's whiskey
½ oz. Rumple Minze peppermint schnapps

Build.

Snake Bite #3

1 part Canadian Club whisky
1 part Hiram Walker peppermint schnapps

Snap Dragon

½ oz. Crown Royal whiskey
½ oz. amaretto
¼ oz. cranberry juice
Splash orange juice

Build.

 GINA GEREMIA • NEW HAVEN, CT

Sneakers

¾ oz. amaretto
¾ oz. pineapple juice
½ oz. vodka

Shake with ice, and strain into a shot glass.

357

Sneeker

½ oz. Bacardi 151 rum
½ oz. Chambord
½ oz. Malibu rum
½ oz. Midori melon liqueur
Splash cranberry juice and 7-Up

Snickers

½ oz. Baileys Irish cream
½ oz. dark crème de cacao
½ oz. Frangelico

Shake with ice, and strain into a shot glass.

Snow Ball

1 oz. Bacardi rum
½ oz. Coco López cream of coconut
½ oz. pineapple juice

Blend with ice and serve.

Snow Cap

½ oz. Sauza tequila
½ oz. Baileys Irish cream

Build.

Snow Drop

1 oz. half-and-half
¼ oz. Cointreau
¼ oz. Galliano
¼ oz. Stolichnaya vodka
¼ oz. white crème de cacao

Shake with ice, and strain into a shot glass.

Snow Melter

¾ oz. Romana sambuca
½ oz. Stubbs rum
½ oz. white crème de cacao

Pour the ingredients into a shot glass.

Snowflake

1 part Hiram Walker peppermint schnapps
1 part Beefeater gin

Build.

Snowshoe

1 ½ oz. Southern Comfort
1 oz. Rumple Minze peppermint schnapps

Build.

So Co Slammer

1 part Southern Comfort
2 parts cola

Build.

S.O.B.

1 ½ oz. Sobieski vodka
½ oz. Marie Brizard blackberry cream
   liqueur

Shake with ice, and serve as a shot.

Sob Sister

1 oz. Sobieski vodka
½ oz. Marie Brizard
½ oz. Marie Brizard blue curaçao

Shake with ice, and serve as a shot.

Soi Sant Neuf Volcano

1 ½ oz. Soi Sant Neuf brandy
Beer to chase

Shoot the Soi Sant Neuf. Follow with a beer chaser.

Son of a Beach

1 oz. Frïs vodka
¾ oz. Hiram Walker blue curaçao
1 oz. 7-Up

Shake the first two ingredients with ice and strain into a shot glass. Top with 7-Up.

Sorry Bastard

1 part Jägermeister
1 part Jose Cuervo tequila

Build.

Sour Apple

¾ oz. Midori melon liqueur
¾ oz. Southern Comfort
Dash sweet and sour mix

Shake with ice, and strain into a shot glass.

Sour Apple Rancher

¾ oz. Midori melon liqueur
¾ oz. Southern Comfort
Daily's sweet and sour mix to fill

 BONNIE MILLER • GREENSBURG, PA

Sour Grapes

½ oz. Chambord
½ oz. Finlandia vodka
½ oz. sweet and sour mix

Shake with ice, and strain into a shot glass.

Sour Lemon

1 ½ oz. sweet and sour mix
1 oz. Frïs vodka
Dash Rose's lime juice

Shake with ice, and strain into a shot glass.

South Beach

1 oz. Southern Comfort
½ oz. DeKuyper Watermelon Pucker
    schnapps
½ oz. orange juice

Shake with ice, and strain into a shot glass.

 KEVIN SCHMITZ • BROWN DEER LANES •
BROWN DEER, WI

South of the Border Root Beer

½ oz. Hiram Walker root beer schnapps
½ oz. tequila
Splash Tabasco

Shake with ice, and strain into a shot glass.

Southern Belle

¾ oz. Baileys Irish cream
¾ oz. Southern Comfort

Shake with ice, and strain into a shot glass.

Southern Butterfly

1 oz. amaretto
1 oz. Southern Comfort
⅛ oz. lime juice

Shake with ice, and strain into a shot glass.

 TEENA • LANEY'S CORRAL • NEWELL, IA

Spanish Fly

1 oz. Sauza Gold tequila
½ oz. Galliano
½ oz. orange juice

Shake with ice, and strain into a shot glass.

Spanish Moss

¾ oz. Kahlúa
½ oz. green crème de menthe
½ oz. Jose Cuervo tequila

Shake with ice, and strain into a shot glass.

Sparkling Raspberry

½ oz. Chambord
1 ½ oz. champagne

Build.

Spasm

1 ½ oz. Disaronno amaretto
½ oz. Kahlúa
½ oz. Baileys Irish cream

Build.

Specimen

1 oz. Finlandia vodka, chilled
½ oz. pineapple juice

Serve in a test tube.

Speed Ball

1 part Jägermeister
1 part Goldschläger
1 part Rumple Minze peppermint schnapps

Build. "If this doesn't get you moving, nothing will."

 JIMMY OPPEL • BOBBY VALENTINE'S SPORTS
GALLERY CAFÉ • MIDDLETOWN, RI

Spider Bite

½ oz. anisette
½ oz. tequila

Build.

Spike

1 part Jose Cuervo tequila
1 part grapefruit juice

Build.

Squirrel's Fantasy

1 oz. amaretto
½ oz. white crème de noyaux
½ oz. Frangelico
Splash club soda

Build. Top with club soda.

 PAT ENSTEN • BRANNIGANS SPORTS BAR AND
GRILL • STILLWATER, OK

Stalactite

1 ⅛ oz. Romana sambuca
¼ oz. Baileys Irish cream
¼ oz. Chambord

Pour sambuca into a cordial glass. Float Baileys
on top. Pour Chambord drop by drop as the top
layer. The Chambord will pull the Baileys through
the sambuca and will settle on the bottom.

Star Wars

1 oz. Southern Comfort
½ oz. Grand Marnier
½ oz. orange juice

Shake with ice, and strain into a shot glass.

Star Wars #2

1 part Grand Marnier
1 part orange juice
1 part sloe gin

Shake with ice, and strain into a shot glass.

Starburst

¾ oz. Malibu rum
½ oz. cranberry juice
½ oz. Finlandia vodka
½ oz. pineapple juice
¼ oz. Chambord

Shake with ice, and strain into a shot glass.

Stars and Stripes

⅓ oz. grenadine
⅓ oz. heavy cream
⅓ oz. blue curaçao

Layer in order in a cordial glass.

Stealth Bomber

½ oz. Baileys Irish cream
½ oz. crème de banana
½ oz. Grand Marnier
½ oz. Kahlúa

Shake with ice, and strain into a shot glass.

Steamboat Special

1 oz. J&B scotch whisky
¼ oz. Grand Marnier

Float Grand Marnier on top and serve.

Stiff Richard

1 part Captain Morgan rum
1 part Damiana liqueur
1 part pineapple juice

Shake and strain over ice, pour into a shot glass.

 VANCE BROWN & MARK TODD • DIAMOND LIL'S
• EUREKA SPRINGS, AR

Stiffed Again

1 ½ oz. B&B liqueur, chilled
Splash club soda

Build.

Stiletto Shooter

⅓ oz. Kahlúa
⅓ oz. peppermint schnapps
⅓ oz. tequila

Build.

Stinger Shooter

⅔ oz. brandy
⅓ oz. white crème de menthe

Shake with ice, and strain into a shot glass.

Stingray

1 ¼ oz. Finlandia cranberry vodka
¼ oz. white crème de menthe

Shake with ice, and strain into a shot glass.

Stinky Pinky

¾ oz. Stolichnaya Ohranj vodka
¾ oz. Stolichnaya Peachnik vodka
½ oz. Cointreau
½ oz. cranberry juice
½ oz. sweet and sour mix

Shake with ice.

Stoli Buster

⅔ oz. Baileys Irish cream
⅔ oz. Stolichnaya vodka

Stir and strain into a shot glass.

Stoli Ohranj Drop

1 ¼ oz. Stolichnaya Ohranj vodka
Orange wedge
Sugar to coat wedge

Serve the vodka with an orange wedge coated in
sugar. Shoot the vodka, then eat the wedge.

Stony

1 oz. Echt Stonsdorfer herbal fruit liqueur

Enjoy icy Echt Stonsdorfer shots straight up.

Stop and Go

1 oz. Finlandia cranberry vodka
½ oz. Midori melon liqueur
⅛ oz. Cointreau
Sugar to rim glass

Chill the ingredients until ice cold. Rim a shot glass with sugar. Layer the ingredients in the above order.

Stop and Go Naked

½ oz. Cointreau
½ oz. lemon juice
¼ oz. Absolut vodka
¼ oz. Bacardi rum
¼ oz. Jose Cuervo tequila
¼ oz. Tanqueray gin
Dash beer

Shake the first six ingredients with ice and strain into a shot glass. Add beer on top.

Storm Cloud

1 oz. Disaronno amaretto
⅓ oz. Bacardi 151 rum
Dash half-and-half

Shake with ice, and strain into a shot glass.

Stormy

¾ oz. Opal Nera black sambuca
½ oz. Grand Marnier
½ oz. half-and-half

Shake with ice, and strain into a shot glass.

Stranded in Tijuana

1 part Bacardi 151 rum
1 part green Chartreuse
1 part Jose Cuervo Especial tequila
1 part sloe gin

Shake with ice, and strain into a shot glass.

Strawberry Blonde

¾ oz. strawberry schnapps
¾ oz. Baileys Irish cream

Build.

Strawberry Quick with a Kick

1 oz. Chambord
1 oz. Tequila Rose
½ oz. Stolichnaya Razberi vodka

 MIKE SICLIANO • SARATOGA SPRINGS, NY

Strip and Go Naked

½ oz. Bacardi 151 rum
½ oz. Stolichnaya vodka
½ oz. sweet and sour mix
¼ oz. cherry brandy
¼ oz. Cointreau

Shake with ice, and strain into a shot glass.

Suicide Blonde

1 oz. Finlandia vodka
½ oz. pineapple juice
Dash Cointreau
Dash lime juice

Shake with ice, and strain into a shot glass.

Sunset

¾ oz. Absolut vodka
½ oz. grenadine
Dash orange juice
Dash 7-Up

Shake the first three ingredients with ice and strain into a shot glass. Add the 7-Up.

Sunset at the Beach

2 oz. pineapple juice
1 ¼ oz. Finlandia cranberry vodka
¼ oz. Midori melon liqueur
¼ oz. raspberry liqueur

Shake with ice, and strain into a shot glass.

Suntan Lotion

1 part Baileys Irish cream, chilled
1 part Captain Morgan Parrot Bay rum, chilled

Mix over ice and strain into a shot glass.

 DENISE DESENA • BAY SHORE, NY

Super Screw or F.S.

1 ¼ oz. Stolichnaya vodka
¼ oz. orange juice
Club soda to top

 RYAN PETERS • WALL, NJ

Supermodel Shot

1 ½ oz. Bacardi Limón
½ oz. Midori melon liqueur
½ oz. blue curaçao

Build.

 BACARDI-MARTINI USA, INC. • MIAMI, FL

Surfers on Acid

¾ oz. Jägermeister
½ oz. Malibu rum
Splash pineapple juice

Build.

 DEBRA WELCH • NEW LONDON, NH

Surfers on Acid #2

1 part Jägermeister
1 part Captain Morgan coconut rum
1 part pineapple juice
Dash grenadine

Build.

Swamp Water

¾ oz. Cointreau
¾ oz. green Chartreuse
½ oz. pineapple juice

Shake with ice, and strain into a shot glass.

Sweaty Irishman!

½ oz. John Jameson & Son Irish whiskey
½ oz. DeKuyper Hot Damn! cinnamon
    schnapps
Dash Tabasco

Build.

 ANGELA PEYTON • ALAMOSA, CO

Swedish Kiss

1 ½ oz. Absolut Kurant vodka
Splash Chambord
Club soda to top

Build first two ingredients. Top with club soda.

Swedish Quaalude

⅓ oz. Absolut vodka
⅓ oz. Baileys Irish cream
⅓ oz. Frangelico

Shake with ice, and strain into a shot glass.

Sweet Lisa

1 oz. Black Haus blackberry schnapps
½ oz. crème de banana
½ oz. Rumple Mintz peppermint schnapps
Splash pineapple juice

Shake with ice, and strain into a shot glass.

 CLAY TARLTON • GALAXY BILLIARDS •
SAN ANTONIO, TX

Sweet Tooth

1 oz. vodka
¼ oz. Cointreau
¼ oz. peach schnapps
Splash cherry brandy
Splash Rose's lime juice

Shake with ice, and strain into a shot glass.

Sweet 'N Tart

1 ½ oz. Absolut Citron
Splash 7-Up
Splash sweet and sour mix
1 tsp. sugar
2 twists lemon
2 twists lime

Garnish with the lemon and lime twists. Makes
two shots.

 ORLANDO V. VILLARREAL, XBAR10DR • UNITED
STATES MARINE CORPS • USS *COMSTOCK* •
SOMEWHERE IN THE WESTERN PACIFIC

Sweetpea

1 part Baileys Irish cream
1 part DeKuyper Buttershots schnapps
1 part Rumple Minze peppermint schnapps

 LOUIE ANDRAKAKOS • COLLEGE PARK, MD

Syracuse Shot

1 ¼ oz. 4 Orange vodka
Splash grenadine

Tame a Monkey

1 part 99 Bananas schnapps
1 part orange juice
1 part pineapple juice
½ part Master of Mixers strawberry dai-
    quiri mix
Touch grenadine

 DORAN VILLNAVE • MASSENA, NY

Tarantula Slammer

1 oz. Sprite
½ oz. Tarantula Reposado tequila

Tart 'N Tangy

1 oz. Bacardi Limón
½ oz. cranberry juice
½ oz. sweet and sour mix
Splash grenadine

Shake with ice, and strain into a shot glass.

 ALBERTO ESCOFFERY • AMHERST, MA

Taxicab

½ oz. Absolut Citron vodka
½ oz. DeKuyper Peachtree schnapps
½ oz. Grand Marnier
½ oz. pineapple juice

Shake with ice, and strain into a shot glass.

 JAMES MONTGOMERY • HOUSTON, TX

TBF

½ oz. Tia Maria
½ oz. Baileys Irish cream
½ oz. Frangelico

Build.

 ROBERT KNAPTON • GUIN BLACK •
LAS VEGAS, NV

T-Bird

1 part Absolut vodka
1 part Grand Marnier
1 part Hiram Walker amaretto
2 ½ oz. pineapple juice
Splash half-and-half (optional)

Shake with ice, and strain into a shot glass.

Tear in my Beer

1 part Absolut Raspberry vodka
1 part blue curaçao
1 part triple sec
1 mug draft beer

Pour the ingredients into a shot glass. Drop the
shot glass into a draft beer and chug.

 JENNA MYERS • REX'S RENDEZVOUS • WARSAW, IN

Teddy Bear

½ oz. root beer schnapps
1 oz. vodka

Layer in a shot glass.

Tequil O'Neil

1 ¼ oz. Tarantula Reposado tequila
¼ oz. orange juice
⅛ oz. club soda

Serve in a shot glass covered with a coaster (preferably in a basketball design) and slam.

Tequila Amigo

1 oz. Jose Cuervo Especial tequila
½ oz. Godiva liqueur
1 oz. heavy cream

Layer in a shot glass.

Tequila Menta

1 oz. Casa Nobel tequila
½ oz. Branca Menta mint liqueur

Serve as a shot.

Tequila Mockingbird Shooter

1 part Swiss chocolate almond liqueur
1 part amaretto
1 part tequila

Build.

Tequila Popper

1 oz. tequila
½ oz. 7-Up

Pour tequila into a shot glass. Fill with 7-Up. Place a napkin over the top of the glass and bang the glass down onto the table. Drink immediately.

Tequila Shot

1 ½ oz. tequila
Pinch salt
Lemon or lime wedge

A premium tequila brand is recommended. Fill a shot glass with the tequila (chilled, if desired). Put the salt between the thumb and index finger of your left hand. While holding the shot glass in your left hand and the lemon or lime wedge in your right, lick the salt and quickly drink the shot of tequila. Suck the lemon or lime immediately afterward.

Tequila Sunrise Shooter

2 parts orange juice
1 part tequila
Splash grenadine

Chill, shake, and strain the first two ingredients
into a shot glass. Drop the grenadine on the top
to give it that sunrise look.

Tequini

1 ½ oz. Sauza Conmemorativo tequila
¼ oz. Martini & Rossi extra dry vermouth

Shake with ice, and strain into a shot glass.

Terminator

½ oz. brandy
½ oz. Kahlúa
½ oz. Wild Turkey bourbon

Build.

Terminator #2

1 part Jägermeister
1 part Southern Comfort

Build.

Test Tube Baby

2 parts strawberry schnapps, chilled
1 part Baileys Irish cream, chilled
1 small Gummi bear

Fill a test tube ¾ with the schnapps, then add the Baileys. Drop the Gummi bear on the top and let it sink to the bottom.

Test Tube Baby #2

¾ oz. amaretto
½ oz. Southern Comfort
1–2 drops half-and-half

Layer Southern Comfort on top of amaretto. Add 1 to 2 drops of half-and-half to the bottom of the drink with a short straw.

Test Tube Baby #3

¾ oz. amaretto
½ oz. tequila
1–2 drops half-and-half

Add 1 to 2 drops of half-and-half to the bottom of the drink with a short straw.

Three Guys from Italy

1 oz. amaretto
1 oz. Borghetti Sambuca
1 oz. Branca Menta

Serve as a shot.

Three Wise Men

1 part Jägermeister
1 part Rumple Minze peppermint schnapps
1 part Bacardi 151 rum

Build.

Three Wise Men Go Hunting

1 part Jack Daniel's whiskey
1 part Jim Beam bourbon
1 part Johnnie Walker scotch
1 part Wild Turkey bourbon

Serve as a shot.

Three-Leaf Clover

1 oz. Baileys Irish cream
¼ oz. Irish Mist liqueur
¼ oz. John Jameson & Son Irish whiskey

Shake with ice, and strain into a shot glass.

Thumper

¾ oz. Courvoisier VSOP cognac
¾ oz. Tuaca

Pour the ingredients over ice and strain into a shot glass.

Thunder and Lightning

1 part Rumple Minze peppermint schnapps
1 part Bacardi 151 rum

Build.

Thunder Cloud

½ oz. Bacardi 151 rum
½ oz. Disaronno amaretto
½ oz. Irish Mist liqueur

Build.

Tic Tac Shooter

1 oz. Metaxa ouzo
1 oz. Rumple Minze peppermint schnapps

Build.

Tickle Me Elmo

1 oz. Bacardi Limón
1 oz. peach schnapps
½ oz. grenadine
½ oz. water

 MICHAEL LONGO • LYNDHURST, NJ

Tidy Bowl

1 ½ oz. vodka
1–2 drops blue curaçao

Build.

Tidy Bowl #2

¾ oz. tequila
½ oz. sweet and sour mix
¼ oz. blue curaçao
¼ oz. Cointreau

Shake with ice, and strain into a shot glass.

Tidy Bowl #3

1 ½ oz. light rum
½ oz. blue curaçao
¼ oz. 7-Up

Mix the first two ingredients and strain into a shot glass. Top with 7-Up.

T.N.T. Cocktail

¾ oz. Hiram Walker anisette
¾ oz. Seagram's V.O. whiskey

Shake with ice, and strain into a shot glass.

To the Moon

½ oz. Bacardi 151 rum
½ oz. Baileys Irish cream
½ oz. Disaronno amaretto
½ oz. Kahlúa

Stir with ice, and strain into a shot glass.

Toasted Almond

¾ oz. Hiram Walker amaretto
¾ oz. Kahlúa
½ oz. cream

Shake with ice, and strain into a shot glass.

Toffee Apple

¾ oz. apple schnapps
¼ oz. butterscotch schnapps

Build.

 WENDY FOSTER • CARNEY'S POINT, NJ

Tomakazi

¾ oz. Beefeater gin
¾ oz. Frïs vodka
½ oz. Rose's lime juice
Splash sour mix
Splash cola

Mix the first four ingredients with ice. Top with
cola.

Tommy Time

1 part Bacardi Limón
1 part Malibu or Captain Morgan Parrot
   Bay rum
1 part orange juice
1 part pineapple juice
Touch grenadine

 TOMMY O'CONNOR • COLLEGE PARK, MD

Tootsie Roll

¾ oz. Mozart chocolate liqueur
¾ oz. Stolichnaya vodka
½ oz. orange juice

Shake with ice, and strain into a shot glass.

Top Banana

1 part Absolut vodka
1 part crème de banana
1 part white crème de cacao

Shake with ice, and strain into a shot glass.

Topshelf

1 oz. Tanqueray gin
½ oz. Grand Marnier
½ oz. orange juice
½ oz. sloe gin

Shake with ice, and strain into a shot glass.

 RORY L. CHATMAN • NORFOLK, VA

Topshelf #2

1 oz. cognac
½ oz. armagnac
¼ oz. Grand Marnier
Splash Bacardi 151 rum
Splash Johnnie Walker Black Label scotch
    whisky
Splash orange juice

 RORY L. CHATMAN • NORFOLK, VA

Torpedo

1 part Carolans Irish cream
1 part Drambuie
1 part tequila

Build.

Torque Wrench

½ oz. champagne
½ oz. Midori melon liqueur
½ oz. orange juice

Build.

Traffic Light

½ oz. sloe gin
½ oz. crème de banana
½ oz. green crème de menthe

Build.

Trailer Trash

1 part DeKuyper Tropical Pineapple
    schnapps
1 part Jose Cuervo tequila
3 drops Rose's lime juice

Line the bottom of a shot glass with lime juice.
Chill the tequila and schnapps. Shake and strain
into a shot glass.

 JENNIFER STRONG • THE FRIENDLY INN •
ASHMORE, IL

Tree Climber

½ oz. Bombay gin
½ oz. sloe gin
½ oz. Stolichnaya vodka
Sweet and sour mix to fill

Shake with ice, and strain into a shot glass.

Tropical Breeze

½ oz. 99 Bananas
½ oz. Bacardi O rum
½ oz. DeKuyper Peachtree schnapps
½ oz. Midori melon liqueur
½ oz. pineapple juice

Shake, strain into a shot glass, and serve.

 JOE JOHNSON • JOE'S CRAB SHACK •
JACKSONVILLE BEACH, FL

Tropical Lifesaver

1 oz. Malibu rum
½ oz. crème de banana
½ oz. pineapple juice

Shake with ice, and strain into a shot glass.

Tropical Tang

1 ½ oz. Bacardi rum
¼ oz. orange juice
¼ oz. pineapple juice
White zinfandel to top

Shake with ice, and strain into a shot glass. Top with white zinfandel.

Tuaca Key Lime Pie

1 ½ oz. Tuaca liqueur
¼ oz. lime juice

Shake with ice, and strain into a shot glass.

Turbo

1 oz. Stolichnaya vodka
½ oz. Hiram Walker apple schnapps
½ oz. Hiram Walker peach schnapps
Splash cranberry juice

Shake with ice, and strain into a shot glass.

Turkey Roaster

1 part Baileys Irish cream
1 part Tia Maria
1 part Wild Turkey 101 bourbon
Half-and-half

Shake with ice, and strain into a shot glass.

 GEORGE • SANTA MONICA, CA

Turkey Shoot

1 ¼ oz. Wild Turkey 101 bourbon
1 ¼ oz. Hiram Walker anisette

Float anisette on top and serve.

Turtle Drop

1 oz. Southern Comfort
½ oz. banana liqueur
Splash cream

Build.

 ANGELA EAGAN • PORTLAND, OR

Tutti Frutti Shot

Stroh Obstler brandy to fill, chilled

Stroh Obstler is available at most German restaurants, or ask your local retailer. Serve in a shot glass.

Twenty-Four 24(K) Nightmare

1 oz. Goldschläger
1 oz. Rumple Minze peppermint schnapps

Build.

Twilight Zone

1 oz. Bacardi rum
½ oz. Myers's Original dark rum
⅛ oz. grenadine

Shake with ice, and strain into a shot glass.

Twin Sisters

½ oz. Bacardi rum
½ oz. Bacardi spiced rum
Dash Coke
Dash lime juice

Build.

 JOHN DOYLE • PHILADELPHIA, PA

Twins Rally

1 oz. blue curaçao
½ oz. Malibu Pineapple rum
½ oz. pineapple juice
Dash grenadine

Shake and strain into a shot glass. Slowly pour in grenadine to make blue and red.

 JAMIE AUERBECK • BREWSKI'S PUB •
WINONA, MN

Twisted Red Licorice

½ oz. vodka
½ oz. sambuca
¼ oz. grenadine
Splash 7-Up

Build.

 GINA GEREMIA • NEW HAVEN, CT

Two-Fifty-Two (252)

1 part Wild Turkey 101 bourbon
1 part Bacardi 151 rum

Build.

Tyson Bites

1 oz. Absolut vodka
1 oz. Southern Comfort
¾ oz. Absolut Kurant vodka
½ oz. Captain Morgan rum
¼ oz. cranberry juice
¼ oz. Malibu rum
¼ oz. orange juice
Splash grenadine
Splash lime juice

Shake with ice, and strain into shot glasses. Makes two (one for each ear).

 RICHIE GOETZ • WEST HAVEN, CT

T-Zone

1 oz. Bacardi 151 rum
1 oz. sloe gin
Splash orange or cranberry juice
Lemon wedge for garnish
Maraschino cherries for garnish

Shake with ice, and strain into a shot glass. Serve with a lemon wedge and maraschino cherries.

 TRACY HARRIS • QUEEN SHEBA LOUNGE •
PHILADELPHIA, PA

U-2

¾ oz. Midori melon liqueur
¾ oz. Rumple Minze peppermint schnapps
¼ oz. Jägermeister

Shake with ice, and strain into a shot glass.

Ultimate 1800 Popper

1 oz. Jose Cuervo 1800 tequila
½ oz. Sprite

Build.

Undertaker

1 oz. Jägermeister
1 oz. Cointreau
⅛ oz. Bacardi 151 rum to float

Build first two ingredients. Float rum on top.

Upper Cut

1 oz. amaretto
1 oz. pineapple juice

Build.

Upside Down Pineapple

2 oz. orange juice
½ oz. Malibu rum
½ oz. Southern Comfort
Dash pineapple juice

Shake with ice, and strain into a shot glass.

Upstarter

1 oz. Galliano
½ oz. Absolut vodka
Dash peach schnapps

Shake with ice, and strain into a shot glass.

Urban Cowboy

½ oz. Southern Comfort
½ oz. Jack Daniel's whiskey

Build.

Urinalysis

2 parts Southern Comfort
1 part Rumple Minze peppermint schnapps

Serve in a test tube for maximum authenticity.

U-Z

½ oz. Baileys Irish cream
½ oz. Irish Mist liqueur
½ oz. Kahlúa

Shake with ice, and strain into a shot glass.

Velvet Hammer

¾ oz. Cointreau
¾ oz. white crème de cacao
½ oz. half-and-half

Shake with ice, and strain into a shot glass.

Velvet Hammer #2

1 part Grand Marnier
1 part half-and-half
1 part Hiram Walker white crème de cacao
1 dash Asbach Uralt brandy

Shake with ice, and strain into a shot glass.

Venetian Blinder

½ shot Galliano
½ shot dark crème de cacao
½ shot half-and-half
Bacardi 151 rum to float

Pour Galliano, crème de cacao, and half-and-half into a shot glass (or layer if you like), and float rum on top.

 MICHAEL RICE, WINNER • GALLIANO BARTENDER
CONTEST • MINNEAPOLIS, MN

Very Berry Kamikaze

½ oz. Cointreau
½ oz. watermelon schnapps
½ oz. wild raspberry liqueur
Dash lime juice

 JOANNE MARTIN • WATERBURY, VT

Viking

1 oz. Galliano
¼ oz. akvavit

Pour Galliano into a shot glass; float the akvavit on top.

Viking Funeral

1 ⅓ oz. Rumple Minze peppermint
    schnapps
⅓ oz. Jägermeister
⅓ oz. Goldschläger

Build.

Vine Climber

¾ oz. Frïs vodka
¾ oz. Midori melon liqueur
½ oz. sweet and sour mix

Shake with ice, and strain into a shot glass.

V.O. Breeze Shooter

¾ oz. Rumple Minze peppermint schnapps
¾ oz. Seagram's V.O.
Splash grenadine

Shake with ice, and strain into a shot glass.

Volcano

1 ¼ oz. Absolut Peppar vodka
Dash Rose's grenadine

Build.

Vulcan Mind Probe

1 oz. Metaxa ouzo
½ oz. Bacardi 151 rum

Build.

Waltzing Matilda

1 oz. Bacardi rum
½ oz. blue curaçao
½ oz. pineapple juice

Shake with ice, and strain into a shot glass.

Wandering Minstrel Shooter

½ oz. Absolut vodka
½ oz. Kahlúa
¼ oz. brandy
¼ oz. white crème de cacao

Shake with ice, and strain into a shot glass.

Warped Willie Shooter

¾ oz. Absolut vodka
¾ oz. Disaronno amaretto
Splash Rose's lime juice

Shake with ice, and strain into a shot glass.

Waterloo

¾ oz. Bacardi rum
¾ oz. Mandarine Napoleon liqueur
½ oz. orange juice

Shake with ice, and strain into a shot glass.

Watermelon

2 parts pineapple juice
1 part Southern Comfort
¾ part Absolut vodka
Splash grenadine

Shake with ice, and strain into a shot glass.

Watermelon #2

1 part Absolut vodka
1 part cranberry juice
1 part Midori melon liqueur

Shake with ice, and strain into a shot glass.

Watermelon #3

2 parts pineapple juice
1 part Midori melon liqueur
1 part Southern Comfort
Splash grenadine

Shake with ice, and strain into a shot glass.

Watermelon Crawl

⅔ oz. sweet and sour mix
⅓ oz. Midori melon liqueur
⅓ oz. vodka

Mix with ice and strain into a shot glass.

 CAROL WELBY & MIKE ADKINS • HAROLD DEAN'S
SADDLE SALOON • PUEBLO, CO

Watermelon Meister

1 shot Jägermeister
Splash DeKuyper Watermelon Pucker
   schnapps

Wave Breaker

¾ oz. Coco López cream of coconut
¾ oz. Finlandia vodka
½ oz. Cointreau
⅛ oz. Rose's lime juice

Blend with ice, and strain into a shot glass.

Wayne's World or 2000 Flushes

½ oz. Bacardi rum
½ oz. blue curaçao
½ oz. Midori melon liqueur
½ oz. Smirnoff vodka
Splash peach schnapps
Splash sweet and sour mix

 WAYNE SPARKS • CARNEY'S PT., NJ

Weasel Water

1 oz. Baileys Irish cream
½ oz. crème de banana
½ oz. half-and-half

Shake with ice, and strain into a shot glass.

Week at the Beach

1 ½ oz. DeKuyper Peachtree schnapps
¼ oz. cranberry juice
¼ oz. Finlandia vodka
¼ oz. orange juice

Shake with ice, and strain into a shot glass.

Wench

¾ oz. Disaronno amaretto
¾ oz. Captain Morgan rum

Build.

Wet Dream

¾ oz. Bacardi rum
¾ oz. crème de noyaux
¾ oz. Malibu Rum
½ oz. pineapple juice

Shake with ice, and strain into a shot glass.

Wet Dream #2

1 part Cointreau
1 part Galliano
1 part orange juice

Shake with ice, and strain into a shot glass.

Wet Spot

1 part Jose Cuervo tequila
1 part Baileys Irish cream

Build.

Whatchamacallit

¾ oz. Frangelico
¾ oz. Tuaca liqueur
¼ oz. Godiva liqueur

 CLAUDE LEVERT • LAS VEGAS, NV

Whiplash

1 part Romana Black sambuca
1 black licorice Twizzler

Put the Twizzler in a test tube, then fill the tube with black sambuca. Refrigerate for 4 hours and let the licorice soak up the liqueur. The proper technique is to drink the shot and chew on the licorice that has been soaking.

Whirly Bird

1 part Chambord
1 part Midori melon liqueur
1 part pineapple juice
1 part Southern Comfort

Shake with ice, and strain into a shot glass.

 ALAN SMITH • BENNIGAN'S •
NEW BRUNSWICK, NJ

Whisker Run

¾ oz. Jack Daniel's whiskey
¼ oz. Coke
3 drops Tabasco
2 pinches black pepper

Build.

 TROY HICKS • BROOKINGS, SD

White Cap Shooter

1 oz. Frangelico
Baileys Irish cream to top

Build.

414

White Delight

½ oz. Dr. McGillicuddy's Mentholmint
    schnapps
½ oz. white crème de cacao

Build.

White Elephant

1 oz. Smirnoff vodka
½ oz. half-and-half
½ oz. white crème de cacao

Shake with ice, and strain into a shot glass.

White Out

¾ oz. Rumple Minze peppermint schnapps
¾ oz. Baileys Irish cream

Build.

White Satin

¾ oz. Tia Maria
½ oz. Frangelico
½ oz. half-and-half

Shake with ice, and strain into a shot glass.

White Spider

1 oz. crème de cacao
1 oz. Stolichnaya vodka

Shake with ice, and strain into a shot glass.

Wicked Stepmother

1 oz. Absolut Peppar vodka
½ oz. Disaronno amaretto

Shake with ice, and strain into a shot glass.

Wild Hawaiian Turkey Shooter

1 oz. orange juice
1 oz. pineapple juice
¼ oz. Disaronno amaretto
¼ oz. Southern Comfort
¼ oz. Wild Turkey 101 bourbon

Shake with ice, and strain into a shot glass.

Wild Thing

1 oz. Finlandia vodka
½ oz. apricot brandy
7-Up to top

Stir the first two ingredients. Top with 7-Up.

Windex

1 part blue curaçao
1 part Absolut vodka

Build.

Woo Woo

¾ oz. DeKuyper Peachtree schnapps
¾ oz. Stolichnaya vodka
½ oz. cranberry juice

Shake with ice, and strain into a shot glass.

Woodstock Shooter

⅓ oz. amaretto
⅓ oz. Bacardi 151 rum
⅓ oz. sweet and sour mix

Shake with ice, and strain into a shot glass.

Woo-Shoo

1 oz. Finlandia cranberry vodka
6 drops peach schnapps

Build.

Yak Milk

⅓ oz. Baileys Irish cream
⅓ oz. Captain Morgan Parrot Bay rum
⅓ oz. crème de cacao

Shake with ice, and strain into a shot glass.

 RYAN NOVAK • MANSFIELD, CT

Yellow Belly C. S.

1 oz. Finlandia vodka
½ oz. cinnamon schnapps
¼ oz. pineapple juice

Shake with ice, and strain into a shot glass.

Yellow Bird

½ oz. Bacardi rum
½ oz. Cointreau
½ oz. Galliano
½ oz. pineapple juice

Shake with ice, and strain into a shot glass.

Yellow Fellow

1 oz. Bombay Sapphire gin
¼ oz. yellow Chartreuse

Shake with ice, and strain into a shot glass.

Yellow Rolls Royce

¾ oz. Baileys Irish cream
¾ oz. Galliano
¾ oz. white crème de cacao

Shake with ice, and strain into a shot glass.

Yellow Rose

1 oz. Finlandia vodka
½ oz. pineapple juice
Beer of your choice

Serve the first two ingredients in a shot glass placed into the center of your favorite beer.

Yellow Snow

1 ½ oz. Finlandia vodka
Splash pineapple juice

Shake with ice, and strain into a shot glass.

Yellow Snow #2

⅓ oz. half-and-half
⅓ oz. Pernod
⅓ oz. white crème de cacao

Shake with ice, and strain into a shot glass.

Yellow Work

1 part Carolans Irish cream
1 part crème de banana
1 part tequila

Build.

You Drive Me Crazy

¼ oz. Bacardi 151 rum
¼ oz. Malibu rum
¼ oz. or less pineapple juice
Grenadine to top

Build the first three ingredients. Top off with grenadine. It will drive ya crazy!

 BARBARA KEHL • WHAT'S UP LOUNGE • HENDERSON, NE

Zimbabwe

1 oz. Absolut Kurant vodka
¼ oz. cranberry juice
¼ oz. grapefruit juice
¼ oz. orange juice
¼ oz. pineapple juice

Shake with ice, and strain into a shot glass.

Zipper

⅓ oz. Grand Marnier
⅓ oz. half-and-half
⅓ oz. tequila

Shake with ice, and strain into a shot glass.

Zipper Dropper

⅓ oz. green crème de menthe
⅓ oz. Kahlúa
⅓ oz. white crème de cacao

Shake with ice, and strain into a shot glass.

Zipperhead

1 part Absolut vodka
1 part Chambord
2 parts club soda

Shake the first two ingredients with ice and strain into a shot glass. Top with soda. Suck up through a straw.

Zombie

3 parts orange juice
3 parts pineapple
1 part Appleton Estate Jamaican rum
1 part apricot brandy
1 part Myers's Original dark rum

Shake with ice, and strain into a shot glass.

YOUR SHOOTER RECIPES

THE DEFINITIVE GUIDE TO SHOT GLASSES

BY MARK PICKVET

Here's the long-awaited sequel to Pickvet's popular book, *Shot Glasses: An American Tradition*. *The Definitive Guide to Shot Glasses* contains much new historical information and line drawings of shot glasses not found in the first book. Hundreds of shot glasses are shown, with little duplication of information or drawings. A helpful glossary and value guide are included. This book is a must for all tumbler collectors. *The Definitive Guide to Shot Glasses* is available directly from Antique Publications. Contact them at:

Antique Publications
P.O. Box 553, Marietta, OH 45750-0553
1-800-533-3433
fax 740-373-6917

Poppers

If you go to a bar and see "exploding" shooters, they've got to be Poppers, one of the many shooter sensations available from Top-Shelf Marketing.

Poppers are specially designed plastic shot glasses with lids. You combine one of the many Poppers recipes, like tequila and champagne or schnapps and seltzer, and put the lid on the Popper. You then slam the Popper on the bar or shake it, and the lid blows off with a loud POP! They're fun, unusual, and inexpensive enough to give away with every drink sale.

George Borrello at Top-Shelf Marketing developed Poppers. In an effort to create something new and unusual, he and his staff came up with the idea of making a tequila slammer with an extra twist. Poppers are similar to tequila slammers, in that you slam them down on the bar, but Poppers blow their tops after slamming, which really draws attention; the disposable shooter glasses make for quick, easy sales.

Poppers are designed to be impulse purchases. The Popper starter kit comes with two hundred Poppers, lids, pour tops, instructions, posters, and a Popper rack so that a server can walk around your establishment and sell directly to your patrons. For more information on Poppers, or for a free sample kit, call Top-Shelf Marketing at 1-800-766-1695, or visit their website at www. top-shelfmarketing.com.

Test-Tube Shooters

The use of test tubes as drink containers originated many years ago in Canada with glass test tubes, but these shooter tubes now come mostly in plastic and in a variety of sizes and colors. Test-tube shooters are now a staple for many bars and have gone from a fad to an accepted medium for serving shots and shooters. The most popular way for bars to serve test-tube shooters is with a specially designated server or shooter girl (or guy). These shooter servers circulate through the crowd and offer patrons a variety of shooters; many of these classic and unusual shot recipes are found in this book.

One of the main sources for test-tube shooters is Top-Shelf Marketing. Using their line of shooter products and this book is a great formula for success in the shooter business. You can call 1-800-766-1695 or visit www.top-shelfmarketing.com.

DRINK INDEX

430

447

ALCOHOL INDEX

452

458

464

465

ABOUT THE AUTHOR

Ray Foley, a former marine with over thirty years of bartending and restaurant experience, is the founder and editor of *Bartender Magazine*. Ray is referred to as "The Legend" for all he has done for bartenders and bartending. *Bartender Magazine* is the only magazine in the world specifically geared toward bartenders and the on-premise and is one of the very few primarily designed for servers of alcohol. *Bartender Magazine* is enjoying its thirty-first year and currently has a circulation of OVER one hundred thousand and is steadily growing.

After serving in the United States Marine Corps and attending Seton Hall University, Ray entered the restaurant business as a bartender, which eventually led to a job as the assistant general manager of The Manor in West Orange, New Jersey, with over 350 employees.

In 1983, Ray left The Manor to devote his full efforts to *Bartender Magazine*. The circulation and exposure has grown from seven thousand to over one hundred thousand to date and has become the largest on-premise liquor magazine in the country.

Ray has been published in numerous articles throughout the country and has appeared on many TV and radio shows.

He is the founder of the Bartender Hall of Fame, which honors the best bartenders throughout the United States, not only for their abilities at bartending but for their involvement and service in their communities as well.

Ray is also the founder of The Bartenders' Foundation Incorporated. This nonprofit foundation has been set up to raise scholarship money for bartenders and their families. Scholarships awarded to bartenders can be used to either further their education or can go toward the education of their children.

Ray is the founder of www.bartender.com (over 1.5 million hits per month) and www.USBartender.com, and many other bar-related websites.

Mr. Foley serves as a consultant to some of our nation's foremost distillers and importers. He is also responsible for naming and creating new drinks for the liquor industry. Here are just a few:

"The Fuzzy Navel"
"The Royal Stretch"—for Grand Royal Oaks Race
"The Royal Turf"—for Grand Royal Oaks Race
"Pink Cadillac"

"Pear-A-Terre"
"Grapeful Red"
"Pear A Mud"
"Pearsian Kat"
"Pomtree Cocktail"
"The Royal Sour"
"The Hamptons "Golden Apfel""
"Mosquito Bite"

Ray has one of the largest collections of cocktail recipe books in the world, dating back to the 1800s and is one of the foremost collectors of cocktail shakers, having 368 shakers in his collection.

He is the author of the following bestsellers:

Bartending for Dummies
Running a Bar for Dummies
The Ultimate Cocktail Book
The Ultimate Little Shooter Book
The Ultimate Little Martini Book
The Ultimate Little Blender Book
Advice from Anonymous
The Best Irish Drinks
Jokes, Quotes and Bartoons
Beer is the Answer...What is the Question?
X-Rated Drinks
Bartender Magazine's Ultimate Bartender's Guide
Vodka 1000
Rum 1000
Tequila 1000
The Best Summer Drinks
God Loves Golfers Best

Ray resides in New Jersey with his wife and partner of 28 years, Jackie, and their son, Ryan.

For additional information or a media kit, please contact:

Jaclyn Foley, Publisher of
Bartender Magazine
Foley Publishing Corporation
PO Box 158, Liberty Corner, NJ 07938
Telephone: (908) 766-6006
Fax: (908) 766-6607
Email: BarMag@aol.com
Website: www.Bartender.com